MOROCCAN
COOKING

ⅢB
BONECHI
Raimage
Raissouni Image

HOW TO READ THE CARDS

DIFFICULTY	FLAVOR	NUTRITIONAL VALUE
● Easy	● Mild	● Low
●● Medium	●● Medium	●● Medium
●●● Difficult	●●● Strong	●●● High

Preparation and cooking times are shown in hours (h) and minutes (e. g. 30' is 30 minutes)

Project: Casa Editrice Bonechi
Series editor: Alberto Andreini
Editor: Paolo Piazzesi
Graphic design: Andrea Agnorelli *and* Maria Rosanna Malagrinò
Layout: Teresa Donato
Editing: Federica Balloni
Translation: Julia Weiss:
Cover: rmalagrino@fuoristudio.it

Chef: Mohammed El Gara *and* Lisa Mugnai
Nutritionist: Dr. John Luke Hili

The photographs illustrating the recipes are the property of the Casa Editrice Bonechi Archives *and were taken by* Andrea Fantauzzo.

Photographs of settings and scenery are the property of the Casa Editrice Bonechi Archives.

The publisher will be grateful for information concerning the sources of photographs without credits and will be pleased to acknowledge them in future editions.

© Copyright by Casa Editrice Bonechi - Firenze - Italia
E-mail: bonechi@bonechi.it

Printed in Italy by Centro Stampa Editoriale Bonechi, Sesto Fiorentino

www.bonechi.com

Distributeur pour le Maroc :
RAIMAGE Sarl.
Angle Rues de Russie et Emsallah
Tél. : 93 42 02, Tanger, Maroc

SPLENDORS AND MAGIC

Moroccan cooking is the splendid expression of a superior gastronomic culture. Over the years it has absorbed and filtered influences from many parts of the world, including distant lands such as Arabia and Persia and developed perfectly balanced dishes with a variety of ingredients, flavors and aromas.

Morocco is one of the world's finest culinary schools. It is not only the international pride of the land of the Atlas mountains where every meal, even the most humble and rushed, is a ritual of reconciliation and thanksgiving, but it is a true heritage of wisdom and skill, one of the most important aspects of its extraordinary civilization, the living proof of its love of art and beauty. Indeed, Moroccan cooking is a refined and generous art, cultivated by the sense of hospitality which is an inborn trait of its people. Each dish that appears on Moroccan tables, even the most humble, is an intelligent preparation using nature's gifts, the results

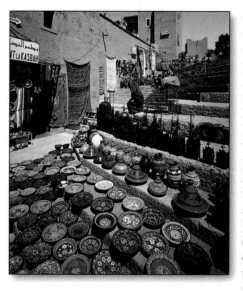

of centuries of refining processes, a feat of edible magic, and a miracle of harmony and pleasure.

Moroccan cooking has a two-thousand year long history. Every people, starting with the Phoenician navigators, that walked on its land left an imprint. It is a compendium of knowledge and techniques of the austere heritage of Berber simplicity, the wealth of the Jewish traditions and refined, cultured legacy of the Arab domination thanks to which the Persian custom of combining meats and fruits, of using spices brought by caravans – starting from cinnamon – the taste for sweet and savory flavors in one dish, and the love of sugar and honey rich sweets have created one of the most remarkable culinary traditions in the world..

Traditional Moroccan gastronomy has a huge range of recipes, preparations and cooking methods: aromatic marinades and appetizing sauces, fresh salads and rich fillings wrapped in crispy dough, hearty soups and seafoods, flavorful roasts and slowly cooked stews. On the whole it is a parsimonious cuisine that wastes nothing, not even time, but it knows how to appreciate waiting, and it uses humble ingredients – if we don't count the luxury of spices – for always sumptuous, spectacular results. Here is an array of dishes that takes us through Morocco's different regions and cultures - city and rural, seaside and mountain and they are often quite different – and brings us the best. The recipes in this book were selected, tested and refined one by one by Mohammed El Gara, expert chef from Rabat. He has a profound knowledge of his country's culinary secrets and thanks to his vast international experience can

Mohammed El Gara, the expert chef from Rabat who has a profound knowledge of Moroccan culinary traditions. Above, a glimpse of Quarzazate with the lively, colored pottery that brightens the village streets.

familiarize European and western audiences with the most authentic Moroccan foods. The text is scattered with his frequent recommendations and suggestions. In Morocco, even if westernization is making major inroads, the methods and tempo of serving food, the types and order of the courses are naturally different from those we find in Europe and the United States. In general, a meal begins with "appetizers" to which Mohammed El Gara dedicates the first section of the book. They may be salads or simple, light hot dishes made with local vegetables: carrots, eggplant and potatoes, peppers, tomatoes and turnips with chickpeas and fava beans, without overlooking olives, garlic and onion that are ever present like green coriander and parsley, and the delicious, juicy salted or natural lemons. On special occasions the simple dishes make way for pastilla a culinary monument that serves to triumphantly introduce an array of extraordinarily appetizing and appealing dishes such as *tajine* that are brought to the table all at once (but you can organize your meals any way you like, even because many Moroccan recipes are one-dish meals). Custom would dictate that foods be eaten with the fingers (thumb, index and middle fingers of the right hand), you are welcome to do so. But if you eliminate the cutlery, be sure to prepare finger bowls with water with lemon and orange flower oil.

And the beverages? Water, or if you like, tea. Given the religious prohibition of alcohol, wine is not served with meals in Morocco. But if you do not have to abide by those rules, you will find that these recipes can be accompanied by some white wines such as Chardonnays or Inzolia from Sicily, as well as some rosés from Puglia that are appropriate with soups and fish. As to the meats, we can suggest nothing better than Tuscan or Sicilian Syrah which is perfect with spicy, aromatic foods.

Morocco is a land of myriad hues, especially those of the wonderful spices that are indispensable in local foods and color all the marketplaces.

MOROCCAN SPICES AND FLAVORINGS

Caraway (*karouiya*) the aromatic seeds of an herbaceous plant from the parsley family; a great aid to digestion.

Cinnamon (*al quarfa*) is the aromatic bark of the *cinnamomum zeyalanicum,* a tropical plant similar to laurel: ground or in sticks it is omnipresent in foods and sweets and is also used with confectioners' sugar to decorate dishes.

Coriander (*al qazbûr*) an herbaceous plant, similar to parsley (*mâdnousse*), its almost inseparable partner in Moroccan culinary tradition; both the leaves and the seeds – which are actually the dried fruits – are used in cooking.

Cumin (*kamoun*) the whole or crushed aromatic seeds of an herbaceous plant from the parsley (and caraway) family. The most commonly found cumin is amber in color, but there are also white and black (the strongest) seeds.

Ginger (*skingher*) the rhizome of *zingiber officinale,* as aromatic and sharp in fragrance as it is in taste; it is available dried and ground in gray and white – which is the finer type.

Macis (*bsibissa*) the reddish rind of the nutmeg, usually dried and ground, with a strongly aromatic bitter flavor.

Mint (*nânâ* or *leqama*) the fragrant, notched leaves are basic ingredients in Moroccan tea, and are also frequently used in cooking.

Nutmeg (*gouza et tib*) the fragment nut of the fruit of *myristica fragrans,* an evergreen from Molucche is now grown in all tropical coastal areas; it is used grated or ground.

Orange flower oil: distilled from orange flower buds, with its fresh fragrance, is widely used in Moroccan pastries as well as other foods. It is sold in most supermarkets.

Saffron (*za'frane*) is obtained in tiny amounts – which explains its astronomical price – from dried crocus pistils; it is widely used in Moroccan cooking in the bright yellow powder, or the purplish-red stems.

Star Anise (*nafâ):* the whole or crushed seeds extracted from the dried, star-shaped fruits of a shrub that originated in China: it has a more intense aroma than green anise.

Sweet paprika (*felfla hloua*): the powder obtained from crushing dried red peppers, it gives warmth and body to Moroccan (and Hungarian) foods and is used in combination with black pepper (*el bzar*); it should not be confused with hot red pepper (*felfla soudania* or *felfla harra*).

Turmeric (*al kharqùm*) from the rhizome of a tropical plant related to ginger, it has a sharp flavor and is orange. It is finely ground to an almost impalpable consistency and is used to flavor and color foods.

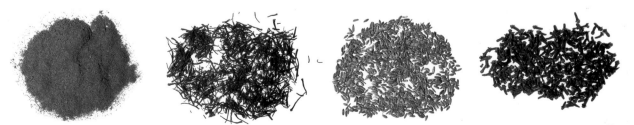

IMPORTANT

The recipes are for 4 or more servings: some are dishes that simply come out better when made in big quantities, others are perfect for fewer persons. The choice is up to the cook – select the menu according to the number of people and remember, many Moroccan recipes create one-dish meals.

Our recipes, especially the more complex ones, are illustrated with step-by-step photos. We recommend that you read the list of ingredients (as well as the preparation, cooking times, level of difficulty, flavor and nutritional values), then read through the whole recipe before you begin. Spiciness is commensurate with Moroccan standards, the foods are rich in condiments and spices. When a recipe calls for a "teaspoon" it should never be heaping, rather use a little less than a level teaspoon. Experience,

the master of life – and cooking – should guide your hand.

As Mohammed El Gara says, "In the kitchen *ainek maisanek* – the eye is your most accurate scale."

A NOTE ABOUT METRICS

These recipes all originated in metric units and conversions can be a problem.

Here the quantities have been rounded up or down according to common sense and convenience. For example, 8 ounces are 225 grams, 200 grams have been converted as 8 ounces as have 250 grams, depending on the ingredients. Cooking is a question of proportions. Oven temperatures are given in both Celsius and Fahrenheit.

THE NUTRITIONIST'S ADVICE

The nutritional features of these foods are identical to what is traditionally known as "Mediterranean cuisine." 1) They contain significant amounts of carbohydrates (at least 50%-60% of the daily calorie intake); they are mainly of the complex type, from durum wheat, rice or other grains such as millet or barley, while the simple sugars come from fruit, honey or sugar. 2) Just about the only seasoning oil is extra virgin olive oil, that is rich in monoleic acid. 3) Proteins are obtained from fish or the so-called "white" meats that are rich in polyunsaturated fats, such as lamb, mutton, and chicken. 4) It has a high fiber content from all the vegetables and legumes that are part of every dish except for the sweets.

To complete the overall nutritional picture, we must mention that this gastronomic tradition is rich in one-dish meals (typical of all nomadic peoples), spices (excellent preservatives that are most useful in places where hot climate makes it difficult to store foods for a long time), honey and sugar used in making sweets (and an excellent source of the quick energy that is so necessary in hot summer weather).

TABLE OF CONTENTS

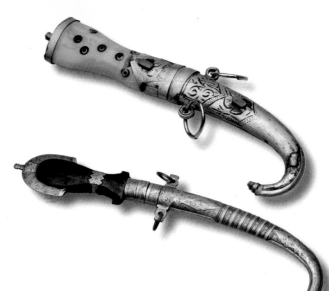

The Kasbah of Ait Benhaddou, a magnificent village that UNESCO has declared part of the World Heritage.

STARTERS

Here are dishes to start a meal ranging from the simple to slightly more elaborate, for everyday or special occasions. We present crispy briouats, savory, fried dumplings– baby brother to the monumental pastilla - with a variety of fillings and a staple at weddings and banquets. And there are fresh, aromatic salads and exquisite vegetables that can be transformed into side dishes for main courses in the following chapters by following the advice of Mohammed El Gara at the bottom of the recipes.

1

BRIOUATS WITH CHEESE AND OLIVES

250 gr/8 oz pastilla dough (see below)

350 gr/13 oz Jiban goat cheese (or other soft, fresh cheese)

150 gr/6 oz black and green olives (pitted)

Coriander (also for garnish)

1 strip salted lemon rind (see page 16)

1 egg and 1 egg white

flour (for the work table)

Salt and pepper

Oil for frying

Servings: 6	
Preparation time: 30'	
Cooking time: 20'	
Difficulty: ●●●	
Flavor: ●●	
Kcal (per serving): 618	
Proteins (per serving): 23	
Fats (per serving): 44	
Nutritional value: ●●●	

1 Wash a nice bunch of coriander and chop it finely with the lemon rind; chop the olives too.
Put the mixture into a bowl, add the crumbled cheese, a little salt and pepper, and the slightly beaten egg (if the egg is small, add a yolk), and mix until thoroughly blended.

2 Cut the dough into 8-10 cm (3–4 inch) wide strips and place them on a floured worktable making sure they don't overlap. Brush a strip with beaten egg white, place a ball of the mixture at the bottom end of the dough, raise the bottom of the dough and fold it to cover the filling.

3 Turn up and then left, folding left and right until you get a triangle, seal by pressing down with your fingers.

4 Repeat until you have used up all the ingredients. Fry a few briouats at a time in lots of hot oil, until golden. Remove with a slotted spoon and drain on paper towels. Serve hot, garnished with sprigs of coriander.

PASTILLA

Pastilla is both a traditional Moroccan dish (see page 25) and the type of unleavened dough used to prepare it, made with flour blended lukewarm water and a dash of salt, worked into thin, soft, elastic sheets (*ouarqa*). Pastilla dates back to the Arab conquest of Morocco. Long ago, every housewife would make the dough herself using a copper disk known as a *tabsil dial ouarqa:* today it is made on a semi-industrial scale.
Tunisian *brik* or Greek *phyllo* dough that are available frozen in most supermarkets are perfect substitutes for *pastilla*.

BRIOUATS WITH SHRIMP

4 Brush a strip of dough with beaten egg white, place a bit of the sautéed shrimp mixture at the bottom end, lift and fold over to cover the filling. Follow the instructions in the preceding recipe, until you use up all the ingredients. Fry a few *briouats* at a time in lots of hot oil until golden. Remove with a slotted spoon and drain on paper towels, serve hot with the garnish of your choice.

250 gr/8 oz pastilla dough
  (see page 10)
400 gr/14 oz precooked,
  shelled shrimp
1 egg white
Flour for the worktable
Olive oil
Oil for frying

For the chermoula:
100 gr/4 oz green olives (pitted)
1 onion
4 cloves garlic
1 bunch green coriander and
  parsley
Ground cumin and sweet
  paprika
1 lemon
Salt and pepper
Olive oil

Servings: 6	
Preparation time: 30'+1h	
Cooking time: 25'	
Difficulty: ●●●	
Flavor: ●●●	
Kcal (per serving): 429	
Proteins (per serving): 14	
Fats (per serving): 26	
Nutritional value: ●●●	

1 Prepare the ingredients: squeeze the lemon. To make the *chermoula* chop the garlic, onion, coriander and parsley together, combine in a bowl with 1/2 teaspoon paprika, salt and pepper; add the lemon juice, 1 tablespoon olive oil and mix to blend.

2 Add the shrimps to the *chermoula*, stir to blend, cover the bowl and refrigerate for 1 hour, mixing now and them. Pour 2 tablespoons olive oil into a skillet, quickly sauté and stir the shrimps and *chermoula* over a lively flame.

3 Cut the *pastilla* dough into 8-10 cm (3-4 inch) wide strips as described in the preceding recipe. Line up the strips on a floured worktable making sure they don't overlap.

BRIOUATS WITH MEAT

250 gr/8 oz pastilla dough
(see page 10)
450 gr/1 lb lean, chopped beef
or veal
1 onion
1 egg and 1 egg white
1 bunch green coriander and
parsley
Ground cinnamon
Sweet paprika
Ginger
Flour for the worktable
Lettuce (for serving)
Salt and pepper
Olive oil
Oil for frying

Servings: 6	
Preparation time: 30'	
Cooking time: 35'	
Difficulty: ●●●	
Flavor: ●●●	
Kcal (per serving): 470	
Proteins (per serving): 21	
Fats (per serving): 28	
Nutritional value: ●●●	

Mohammed El Gara tells us that *briouats* can be made in cylinders as well as triangles, in fact, both shapes are often seen on the same platter. Clean and chop the onion, wilt it slowly in a skillet with 4 tablespoons olive oil. After about 4 minutes add the meat, season with salt and pepper, stir in 1 teaspoon paprika, brown and stir over a moderate flame for ten minutes. Put the meat into a bowl, add the chopped coriander and parsley, 1/2 teaspoon cinnamon and a pinch of ginger; add the slightly beaten egg and blend. Cut the dough into 8 by 15 cm (3 by 6 inch) rectangles (following the instructions in the preceding recipes). Place a spoonful of the meat mixture on a rectangle, roll up, seal the edge and brush with beaten egg white. Repeat until you have used up all the ingredients. Fry a few *briouats* at a time in lots of hot oil until golden. Remove with a slotted spoon, drain on paper towels and serve on a bed of lettuce. Or according to the strictest Moroccan tradition, serve sprinkled with cinnamon and confectioners' sugar.

Fava Bean
Croquettes

250 gr/8 oz dried fava beans 1 onion 1 clove garlic 1 bunch parsley Flour Cumin 1/2 sachet /1/2 oz/ 1 tablespoon baking powder Green salad Salt and pepper Olive oil Oil for frying	

Servings: 4-6	
Preparation time: 20'+20'+6h	
Cooking time: 20'	
Difficulty: ●●	
Flavor: ●●●	
Kcal (per serving): 384	
Proteins (per serving): 9	
Fats (per serving): 26	
Nutritional value: ●●●	

1 Clean the beans by removing the thin skin and soak in water for at least 6 hours before using. Drain and put them through the blender along with the sliced onion, peeled garlic, 1 sprig parsley, 1 teaspoon cumin, 1 tablespoon baking powder (this will make the croquettes "lighter"), 1 teaspoon olive oil and salt and pepper.

2 Put the mixture into a bowl, if necessary thicken with a few tablespoons of flour. Coat your hands with flour to prevent sticking, take a tablespoon of the mixture and shape it into a walnut-size ball;

roll in flour and then set aside for about 20 minutes. Fry in lots of hot oil, remove when golden, drain on paper towels and serve on a bed of green salad.

MIXED SALAD

4 ripe tomatoes
1 onion
1 cucumber
1 green pepper
1 sprig parsley (for garnish)
1 lemon
Salt and pepper
Olive oil
Servings: 4
Preparation time: 20'
Cooking time:
Difficulty: ●
Flavor: ●●
Kcal (per serving): 145
Proteins (per serving): 3
Fats (per serving): 10
Nutritional value: ●●

Wash, clean and dry the vegetables; squeeze the lemon. In a bowl combine the tomatoes, cut into circles, the peeled cucumber, also cut into round slices, the green pepper cut into narrow strips (be sure to remove the seeds and white rib). Add the onion sliced into rings and a sprig of chopped parsley. Prepare the dressing: combine 3 tablespoons olive oil with the lemon juice (or vinegar if you prefer), salt and pepper. Toss the salad and serve as a refreshing *entremets* between the savory courses of a traditional Moroccan meal.

SALTED LEMONS

Lemons, and in particular salted lemons, are a common ingredient in our recipes. To prepare, them, make a slit in the peel and stuff with coarse sea salt. Put the lemons into a jar, cover with lukewarm water; seal the jar and store in a dark place for about one month. Mohammed El Gara recommends that you try this – they give foods an incomparable fresh fragrance – using lemons with a thin skin and delicate aroma.

PEPPER AND TUNA SALAD

Cook the eggs for 7 minutes until hardboiled and peel. Squeeze the lemon, wash the peppers and roast them in the oven, remove the skins and seeds and cut them into strips. Combine the chopped onion and garlic in a salad bowl. Crush the cumin in a mortar with a pinch of salt then transfer it to the salad bowl, then add the peppers and tomatoes, cut into wedges, the coarsely chopped eggs, chopped olives and the drained, crumbled tuna fish. Prepare the dressing by combining the lemon juice with 4-5 tablespoons olive oil. Pour over the salad, toss and serve.

200 gr/8 oz tuna fish, oil pack
2 bell peppers
2 tomatoes
2 eggs
1 onion
1 clove garlic
1 dozen black olives (pitted)
1 lemon
Cumin seeds
Salt and pepper
Olive oil

Servings:	4
Preparation time:	30'
Cooking time:	12'
Difficulty:	●
Flavor:	●●
Kcal (per serving):	423
Proteins (per serving):	39
Fats (per serving):	24
Nutritional value:	●●

CARROT SALAD

4 young carrots
3 cloves garlic
1 shallot
1 lemon
Sugar
Ground cumin
Orange flower oil
Orange peel, sliced thinly
    olives and parsley
    (for garnish)
Salt and pepper
Olive oil

Servings:	4
Preparation time:	20'+ 1h
Cooking time:	10'
Difficulty:	●
Flavor:	●
Kcal (per serving):	130
Proteins (per serving):	1
Fats (per serving):	10
Nutritional value:	●●

Squeeze the lemon. Peel the carrots, cut into circles and scald in lightly salted boiling water for 10 minutes along with the peeled garlic. Drain, discard the garlic and put carrots into a bowl with the chopped shallot. Combine 4 tablespoons olive oil with the lemon juice and 1 tablespoon orange flower oil, 1 teaspoon sugar, 1 pinch of cumin and a dash of pepper. Pour over the carrots, toss and serve at room temperature. In summertime, refrigerate for 1 hour before serving. Decorate the salad with sliced orange peel, olive circles and parsley: try it with *sardine tahine* (page 63) or other fish dishes.

EGGPLANT SALAD

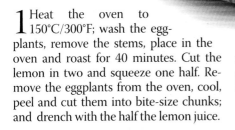

1 Heat the oven to 150°C/300°F; wash the eggplants, remove the stems, place in the oven and roast for 40 minutes. Cut the lemon in two and squeeze one half. Remove the eggplants from the oven, cool, peel and cut them into bite-size chunks; and drench with the half the lemon juice.

2 Peel and crush the garlic and sauté it gently in a skillet with 4 tablespoons olive oil, add the eggplants, the tomatoes cut into pieces, the rest of the lemon juice, salt and pepper, 1 teaspoon paprika and a pinch of hot pepper. Cook covered for 20 minutes, remove the lid and cook 10 minutes more. Serve lukewarm or cold garnished with black olives, the other half lemon sliced and parsley.

In Morocco Zaalouk, *an eggplant and tomato paste is made with more or less the same ingredients and it is usually served with appetizers; it is also delicious with lamb.*

---

1 kg/2 lbs eggplant
250 gr/8 oz ripe tomatoes
3 cloves garlic
Sweet paprika
Ground (or fresh) hot red pepper
1 lemon (also for garnish)
1 dozen black olives and parsley (for garnish)
Salt and pepper
Olive oil

Servings: 6
Preparation time: 15'
Cooking time: 30'+ 45'
Difficulty: ●●
Flavor: ●●
Kcal (per serving): 133
Proteins (per serving): 3
Fats (per serving): 10
Nutritional value: ●●

TOMATOES STUFFED WITH RICE

1 Prepare all the ingredients: wash the tomatoes, cut off the tops and set them aside. Scoop out the insides, salt lightly and turn the tomatoes upside down and let them drain.

2 Gently sauté the sliced onion and carrot (cubed) in a skillet with 4 tablespoons olive oil and a pinch of ginger for about 20 minutes.

3 Boil the rice in the vegetable broth (about 20 minutes), drain, put into a bowl, add a squiggle of olive oil and set aside to cool. Squeeze the lemon and save a bit of the skin.

4 Thinly slice the radishes, add them to the rice along with sautéed onions and carrots, chopped parsley, grated lemon zest and lemon juice, a pinch each of salt and hot pepper. Stuff the tomatoes with the rice mixture and refrigerate for 2-3 hours, then put on the "lids" and serve. Mohammed El Gara says that this is an excellent dish on hot summer days!

To make vegetable broth simmer 1 carrot, 1 onion, 1 stalk celery and 1 small tomato in lightly salted water for 30 minutes; or, you can use granulated vegetable bouillon.

4 ripe tomatoes
300 gr/12 oz long grain
    (Basmati or similar) rice
1 onion
1 carrot
1 sprig parsley
4 radishes
Ground ginger
Ground hot red pepper
1 lemon
Vegetable broth (see below)
Salt and pepper
Olive oil

Servings: 4	
Preparation time: 30'+ 2-3h	
Cooking time: 40'	
Difficulty: ●●	
Flavor: ●●	
Kcal (per serving): 418	
Proteins (per serving): 7	
Fats (per serving): 11	
Nutritional value: ●●	

BAKED TOMATOES

4-5 firm, ripe tomatoes
Sugar
Salt and pepper
Olive oil

Servings:	4
Preparation time:	20'
Cooking time:	1h 30'
Difficulty:	●
Flavor:	●●
Kcal (per serving):	126
Proteins (per serving):	1
Fats (per serving):	10
Nutritional value:	●●

1 Scald the tomatoes in boiling water for 5 minutes. Drain, peel, cut in half and remove the seeds. Season with salt and pepper. Grease a baking dish with olive oil and arrange the tomatoes in it, round side up.

2 Sprinkle with 2 teaspoons sugar, and a squiggle of olive oil. Bake in a slow oven (preheated to 120°C/250°F) for 1 and 1/2 hours. Serve lukewarm, perhaps as a side dish with the kebabs on pages 108-109. If you prefer to avoid sweet-and-sour flavors, season with a mixture of chopped garlic, coriander, parsley and a pinch of cumin instead of the sugar.

SCRAMBLED EGGS WITH SHRIMP

1 Wash the tomatoes and cut them into chunks; wash the peppers, eliminate the seeds and cut them into chunks too. Gently sauté the vegetables in a skillet with 4 tablespoons olive oil, the finely chopped garlic, salt and pepper.

2 In the meantime, scald the shrimp in lightly salted boiling water, remove the heads, shells and the black vein. Turn them into the skillet and cook over a low flame for 5 minutes. Break the eggs into the skillet, stir quickly, salt to taste and serve immediately with a sprinkling of chopped parsley.

16 shrimp
4 eggs
2 tomatoes
2 fresh, small green peppers
2 cloves garlic
Parsley
Salt and pepper
Olive oil

Servings: 4	
Preparation time: 15'	
Cooking time: 30'	
Difficulty: ●	
Flavor: ●●	
Kcal (per serving): 345	
Proteins (per serving): 33	
Fats (per serving): 20	
Nutritional value: ●●	

FISH PASTILLA

550 gr/1 1/4 lbs pastilla dough
(see page 10), (13 sheets)
700 gr/ 1 1/2 lbs codfish fillets
(or other firm, white fish)
500 gr/1 lb baby squid,
cleaned and cut into rings
500 gr/1 lb shelled shrimp
8 giant prawns, whole
6 cloves garlic
2 bell peppers
1 bunch green coriander and
parsley (also for garnish)
2 bay leaves
2 egg yolks
Sweet paprika
Ground hot pepper and
powdered saffron
Flour
1 piece salted lemon rind (see
page 16)
1/2 lemon (plus 1 whole lemon
for garnish)
Salt and pepper
Olive oil

Servings: 8-10	
Preparation time: 30'	
Cooking time: 30'	
Difficulty:	●●●
Flavor:	●●●
Kcal (per serving): 440	
Proteins (per serving): 31	
Fats (per serving): 16	
Nutritional value:	●●

1 Prepare the ingredients; squeeze the half lemon. Cut the fish into chunks and sauté in a skillet with a little oil, together with the shrimps and the finely chopped salted lemon rind. Add 1 glass hot water, cover and cook over a lively flame, stirring occasionally. Turn off the flame, add the lemon juice and cool. In the meantime cut the squid into rings; in a saucepan combine with 1 glass water, the peppers cut into strips and the bay leaves and scald for 10 minutes. Drain the squid and peppers, discard the bay leaves, strain the liquid and set it aside.

2 In a mortar (or blender) reduce the peeled peppers, peeled garlic, chopped coriander and parsley, 1 tablespoon paprika, and a pinch each of hot pepper and saffron to a paste, dilute with a little of the broth from the squid. Put the mixture into a bowl, add the fish, shrimp and squid, season with salt and pepper and stir. Beat the egg yolks with 1 teaspoon flour, this will be your "glue" to hold the dough together. Heat the oven to 180°C/350°F.

3 Grease a round baking pan (40 cm/ 16 inches in diameter, and not more than 2.5 cm/1 inch deep) with olive oil. Arrange 3 sheets of the pastilla dough on the bottom so that they overlap slightly and come up over the edges of the pan. Brush with the egg and flour mixture.
Lay another 4 sheets of dough, brushed with the egg mixture, on top, perpendicularly to the first three; they too should hang over the edges of the pan. Now, spread the filling evenly on top.

4 Fold the edges over to wrap the filling and brush. Now brush another 3 sheets of dough, lay them on top, with the edges hanging over the pan; brush the last 3 sheets, put them on top, perpendicularly.

Tuck the well-brushed ends of the top 6 sheets under the "package" pressing firmly to seal. Bake for 10 minutes. Remove from the oven, put the clean whole prawns on top, and return to the oven to brown under the grill for another 10 minutes. Serve the *pastilla* garnished with lemon slices and sprigs of parsley (or to be traditional, sprinkled with cinnamon and confectioners' sugar).

Almost a piece of beautiful embroidery, the pastilla hides a tasty filling inside the crispy decorated shell, offering all the refinement of Moroccan cuisine. No traditional meal, especially if it is to celebrate a wedding or other happy event, can be considered complete without a monumental pastilla filled with squab, giblets, chicken (like the next recipe), that brilliantly blends sweet and savory flavors, or fish. Pastilla is the important prelude to the main courses, but for European and western palates it can be a one-dish meal. Mohammed El Gara suggests that if the sheets of dough are too dry to bend and tuck, brush them with a little melted butter, and stagger them, like flower petals to make folding them under easier.

CHICKEN AND ALMOND PASTILLA

600 gr/21 oz pastilla dough
(see page 10), (14 sheets)
1 chicken, ready to cook,
about 1.6 kg/ 3 1/2 lbs
8 eggs and 2 yolks
460 gr/1 lb shelled, blanched
almonds (also for garnish)
3 onions
1 bunch of green coriander
and parsley, tied together
1 slice salted lemon
(see page 16)
Ground cinnamon
Powdered saffron and stems
2 sticks cinnamon
15gr/1/2 oz/ 1 tablespoon flour
Confectioners' sugar (for
garnish)
Salt and pepper
100 gr/4 oz butter

Servings: 8-10	
Preparation time: 30'	
Cooking time: 1h 20'	
Difficulty: ●●●	
Flavor: ●●●	
Kcal (per serving): 1075	
Proteins (per serving): 50	
Fats (per serving): 67	
Nutritional value: ●●●	

1 Clean the onions. Cut the chicken into pieces and brown in a saucepan with 40 gr/1 1/2 oz melted butter, a chopped onion, the coriander and parsley bouquet, cinnamon sticks, and a pinch each of saffron stems and powdered saffron. After 10 minutes add enough hot water to cover the chicken; put on the lid and cook over a low flame.
When the chicken is tender, remove it from the pan, bone and cut up the meat. Chop the other 3 onions and put them into the pan with the drippings along with the salted lemon, cover and simmer slowly for 15 minutes, add the chicken, season with salt and pepper, add 1 tablespoon ground cinnamon and stir to combine the flavors.

2 Strain the contents of the pan; put the chicken and onions aside and keep warm. Heat the strained liquid in a large skillet, beat the eggs lightly with salt and pepper and pour into the skillet. Stir so that the eggs set; set aside and keep warm.
Toast the almonds in a dry non-stick pan, set a few aside for garnish and coarsely chop the rest. Beat the two eggs with the flour to make the paste. Heat the oven to 180°C/350°F.

3 Butter a round baking pan (40 cm/ 16 inches in diameter); brush 3 sheets of dough with the egg and flour mixture and arrange them in the bottom of the pan, with the edges hanging over the side; brush the next 3 sheets, put them on top, perpendicularly. Sprinkle the chopped almonds over the dough.

4 Cover with 2 sheets of brushed dough, and place the chicken, onion and eggs on top. Wrap the overhanging dough over the filling and brush so they will stick together. Cover with the last 6 sheets of egg-brushed dough tucking the edges under as in the above recipe. Sprinkle with melted butter and bake for 10 minutes, then brown under the grill for another 10. Serve the *pastilla* sprinkled with cinnamon, confectioners' sugar and chopped almonds.

SESAME BREAD

500 gr/1 lb flour
25 gr/1 oz brewer's yeast
Sugar
Sesame seeds
Salt

Servings: 4	
Preparation time: 30'	
Cooking time: 30'	
Difficulty: ●●	
Flavor: ●●	
Kcal (per serving): 463	
Proteins (per serving): 11	
Fats (per serving): 1	
Nutritional value: ●●	

Dilute the yeast in a cup of lukewarm water with a teaspoon of sugar. Cover the cup and set aside for 20 minutes. Sift the flour together with 1 tablespoon salt; mound the flour on your work table and make a well in the middle. Add the diluted yeast and knead, add enough water to make a smooth dough. Divide the dough into 3 equal parts and shape into 3 round, flat loaves. Sprinkle with sesame seeds. Place the loaves on a floured oven pan and cover with a cloth. Let rise for 1 hour. Remove the cloth and bake at 220°C/400°F for 30 minutes.

Bread is served with every Moroccan meal, be it is simple or important, and there are still many families, specially in the countryside, that bake their own. The loaves are usually round and the bread is not only an accompaniment, but is often used to help fingers bring food to the mouth, especially when there are sauces or dips. Sometimes a little garlic is added to the dough. In addition to "normal" bread, there are types flavored with sesame, anise, cumin or caraway seeds.

Soups
and Potages

The undisputed protagonist of this chapter is harira, the dish that is used to break the Ramadan fast at sunset, with its animal and vegetable proteins as well as fiber and carbohydrate content along with sweet baghrir and honeyed fritters known as shebbakia. Then, late at night comes the big meal. Many people eat harira in the morning as soon as they wake up to build an energy reserve for the rest of the day. Along with harira – in more "sophisticated" versions as well - this section include a selection of soups. Whether they be from the seaside or mountains, city or country, hearty or delicate they are all delicious.

2

Bissara Puréed Fava Beans

200 gr/8 oz dried fava beans
4 cloves garlic
2 lemons
Ground hot red pepper
Ground cumin
Salt and pepper
Olive oil

Servings:	4
Preparation time:	20' + 6h
Cooking time:	1h 10'
Difficulty:	●
Flavor:	●●
Kcal (per serving):	268
Proteins (per serving):	11
Fats (per serving):	12
Nutritional value:	●●

Squeeze one lemon. Soak the fava beans in water for at least 6 hours, drain and put in a pot with 2 liters /2 quarts water, 4 tablespoons olive oil and the peeled garlic. When the water boils, cover the pot and cook over a medium flame for 30 minutes. Drain the beans, leaving the water in the pot and put them through the blender or food mill and return to the pot, add the lemon juice and a pinch of salt. Stir and cook slowly until it acquires the consistency of a *velouté*. Serve the *Bissara* sprinkled with cumin and hot pepper, with lemon wedges on the side.

TADAFFI

Peel the garlic; ready the peppermint and other herbs for use. Fill a pot with 2 liters/2 quarts water, add a pinch of salt, the mint leaves (leave a few for garnish), oregano, thyme, cinnamon and 1 teaspoon saffron stems. Bring to the boil and cook slowly for 10 minutes. When the garlic is tender remove all 6 cloves, drain and crush to a paste. Return the garlic to the pot and boil slowly for 5 minutes more. Gradually add the semolina stirring vigorously and cook for another 5 minutes while stirring. Garnish with mint leaves and serve hot with a dash of freshly ground pepper and the dates on the side.

200 gr/8 oz semolina
6 cloves garlic
1 bunch fresh peppermint
   leaves (also for garnish)
Fresh thyme and oregano
1 stick cinnamon
Saffron stems
100 gr/4 oz dates
Coarse salt and peppercorns
Olive oil

Servings: 4	
Preparation time: 10'	
Cooking time: 25'	
Difficulty: ●	
Flavor: ●●	
Kcal (per serving): 337	
Proteins (per serving): 7	
Fats (per serving): 10	
Nutritional value: ●●	

CHORBA

1 kg/2 lbs assorted fish
   (grouper, weaver, mullet,
   smooth hound, etc.)
3-4 tomatoes
1 bell pepper
1 onion
2 cloves garlic
2 hot red peppers
Cumin
Bread
Salt
Olive oil

Servings: 4	
Preparation time: 25'	
Cooking time: 1h	
Difficulty: ●●	
Flavor: ●●●	
Kcal (per serving): 507	
Proteins (per serving): 39	
Fats (per serving): 18	
Nutritional value: ●●●	

1 Clean the fish, cut into pieces and set aside. Peel and finely chop the onion and garlic; sauté in a saucepan with 4-5 tablespoons olive oil, 1 teaspoon cumin and the chopped hot red peppers.

2 Add the tomatoes, cut into chunks, salt and pepper; cook slowly for about 15 minutes.

3 Clean the bell pepper, remove the stem and seeds and cut it into strips; add it to the pan, stir and cook 7-8 minutes more.

4 Add 1 liter/1 quart water, the fish and a dash of salt. Cover and cook slowly for about 30 minutes. Strain the broth through a sieve, put the fish into it and serve the *chorba* piping hot with bread croutons.

Harira

400 gr/14 oz lean beef for stew
250 gr/8 oz dried chickpeas
100 gr/4 oz lentils (or barley)
6 ripe tomatoes
1 big onion
1 stalk celery
100 gr/4 oz fidelini (or other
  similar noodles)
6 eggs
Saffron stems
Ground ginger
1 bunch green coriander
  and parsley
Tomato concentrate
50 gr/ 1 1/2 oz flour
1 lemon
Milk (optional)
Dates and dried figs
Salt and pepper
10 gr/ 2 teaspoons butter

Servings: 6	
Preparation time: 25'+ 8h	
Cooking time: 1h 30'	
Difficulty: ●●	
Flavor: ●●●	
Kcal (per serving): 547	
Proteins (per serving): 41	
Fats (per serving): 15	
Nutritional value: ●●	

1 Before you begin soak the chickpeas in water for at least 8 hours. Prepare the herbs and vegetables for use. Cut the meat into bite-size pieces and then put it into a pot with the butter, chickpeas, lentils, chopped onion, diced celery and a pinch each of ginger, saffron, salt and pepper. Add 2 liters/2 quarts cold water, cover the pot; bring to the boil, then lower the flame and cook slowly for at least 1 hour.

2 In the meantime, wash the tomatoes and put them through a food mill; collect the pulp and juice in a bowl. When the hour is up, add the tomato to the pot with another 1/2 liter/1 pint boiling water, the coriander and parsley. Season to taste with salt and pepper. When it reaches the boil cover and cook for about 15 minutes.

3 While the pot is simmering, cook 4 eggs for 7 minutes, until hard. Cool and shell. Dissolve the flour in a little hot water with 2 tablespoons tomato concentrate. Remove the pot from the stove, stir in the tomato and flour mixture; put the pot back on the stove. Cook and stir, uncovered, over a low flame for another 10 minutes.

4 Add the noodles broken up and cook until they are *al dente*; remove the pot from the stove and beat in the other two eggs. *Harira* is traditionally served hot with hardboiled eggs sprinkled with cumin, with dates, figs, and fresh lemon on the side. The preferred beverage is milk.

Harira with Pigeon

4 pigeons ready to use
400 gr/14 oz peeled, blanched
  almonds
2 onions
35 gr/1 oz flour
1 lemon
1 bunch green coriander
  and parsley
Saffron stems
Ground Cinnamon
Salt and pepper
Olive oil

Servings:	8
Preparation time:	15'
Cooking time:	1h 30'
Difficulty:	●●●
Flavor:	●●●
Kcal (per serving):	566
Proteins (per serving):	26
Fats (per serving):	43
Nutritional value:	●●●

Cut the pigeons in half. Finely chop the coriander and parsley. Squeeze the lemon, clean and chop the onions. Put the onions into a pot with the almonds, 1 teaspoon cinnamon and a pinch of saffron, the parsley and half the coriander, and 1 tablespoon olive oil. Add 1 1/2 liters/ 1 1/2 quarts water, cover and bring to the boil, lower the flame and boil 15 minutes longer.
Add the pigeons, put the lid back on the pot and cook slowly until the meat is tender, add 1 1/2 liters/1 1/2 quarts hot water, when it boils again season with salt and pepper. Add the rest of the chopped coriander and simmer for 5 minutes more.
In the meantime, dissolve the flour in a cup of hot water, stirring so that there are no lumps. Remove the pot from the stove, blend in the flour, return to the stove and bring to the boil, stirring all the while. After about 15 minutes, add the lemon juice. Serve the *harira* hot, with 1/2 pigeon for each guest. This is a specialty of Marrakech, and is actually a one dish meal. Sometimes veal kidneys are used instead of pigeon.

TROTTER SOUP

Before you begin, soak the chickpeas for at least 8 hours. Rinse the trotter and scald it in boiling water for 15 minutes; drain and dry. Brown the trotter in a saucepan with 4 tablespoons olive oil, a dash each of salt and pepper and 1 teaspoon turmeric. Add the drained chickpeas and cover with water. When it boils lower the flame cover the pot and simmer slowly for about 1 1/2 hours. In the meantime cook the eggs for 7 minutes (until they are hardboiled), shell and chop. Remove the trotter from the broth, bone and cut the meat into strips. Put the meat back onto the pot with the chickpeas and reheat the soup to serving temperature (it should be hot). Sprinkle with chopped egg and serve. Considering its high protein content, this is actually a one-dish meal.

1 calf's trotter
200 gr/8 oz dried chickpeas
2 eggs
Ground turmeric
Salt and pepper
Olive oil

Servings:	4
Preparation time:	20'+ 8h
Cooking time:	2h
Difficulty:	●●
Flavor:	●●
Kcal (per serving):	420
Proteins (per serving):	36
Fats (per serving):	18
Nutritional value:	●●

LEGUME SOUP

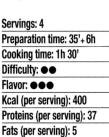

1 Before you begin soak the legumes as needed (that is the beans and fava beans). Drain and put them into a saucepan with the meat cut into chunks and the chopped onion.

2 Cover with cold water (about 1 1/2 liters/ 1 1/2 quarts), put on the lid and start cooking. When it reaches the boil, lower the flame and simmer for 30 minutes: add salt, pepper, and a pinch each of cinnamon and turmeric, and simmer for another 30 minutes.

3 Add the vegetables, washed, peeled and diced. Add enough hot water to bring it to the desired consistency and cook covered for 30 minutes more. Serve the soup piping hot topped with the chopped herbs, thinly sliced onion and drained pickled vegetables. Like the above recipe, this is a protein rich food and it has even more fiber so it is an ideal one-dish meal.

250 gr/8 oz mixed dried
   legumes (fava beans, peas,
   beans, lentils)
400 gr/14 oz lean lamb
2 ripe, firm tomatoes
1 small onion
1 small eggplant
1 bell pepper
1 potato
Ground cinnamon and turmeric
Salt and pepper

For serving:
1 bunch of fresh herbs
   (coriander, watercress,
   parsley and mint)
4 green onions
   vegetables pickled in vinegar

Servings: 4	
Preparation time: 35'+ 6h	
Cooking time: 1h 30'	
Difficulty: ●●	
Flavor: ●●●	
Kcal (per serving): 400	
Proteins (per serving): 37	
Fats (per serving): 5	
Nutritional value: ●●	

PURÉED CHICKPEAS

700 gr/ 1 1/2 lbs lean beef
1 shank bone with the marrow
500 gr/1 lb dried chickpeas
1 onion
2 potatoes
3 cloves garlic
1 bunch green coriander (also for garnish)
Ground turmeric
Saffron stems
Salt and pepper
Olive oil

Servings: 4	
Preparation time: 20'	
Cooking time: 2h	
Difficulty: ●●	
Flavor: ●●●	
Kcal (per serving): 776	
Proteins (per serving): 66	
Fats (per serving): 18	
Nutritional value: ●●●	

1 Before you begin, soak the chickpeas for 8 hours. Clean the vegetables, Peel and cube the potatoes. Put the meat, bone, drained chickpeas, peeled and crushed garlic, the onion cut into wedges and the potatoes into a large pot.

2 Add one teaspoon saffron stems, a few sprigs of coriander and 5 tablespoons olive oil, cover with water and put on the lid. When it comes to the boil lower the flame and simmer for about 90 minutes.

3 Remove the meat and bone from the pot, drain the chickpeas and vegetables (the potatoes will have practically dissolved); save the cooking liquid. Put the solids through a food mill and return to the pot with the broth, the meat and bone. You may have to add a little more hot water to get the right amount of soup.

4 Add a few more sprigs of coriander and 1 teaspoon turmeric, season with salt and pepper. Cover and simmer for 30 minutes. Serve this nice, thick soup garnished with coriander, with the meat as the main dish, and olive oil on the side for dressing. This recipe from the rich Moroccan Jewish tradition offers both the first and main course. Remember that the rules for preventing BSE - or "mad cow disease" permit using and eating bone marrow, it is the medulla or spinal cord that is forbidden.

BARLEY SOUP

200 gr/8 oz cracked pearl
   Barley (or barley meal)
1 onion
1/2 liter/ 1 pint milk
2 cloves garlic
Fresh thyme (also for garnish)
Salt and pepper
Olive oil

Servings: 4	
Preparation time: 10'	
Cooking time: 45'	
Difficulty: ●●	
Flavor: ●●	
Kcal (per serving): 360	
Proteins (per serving): 10	
Fats (per serving): 15	
Nutritional value: ●●	

This is a simple, energy rich soup from the Berber tradition. Clean and chop the onion and garlic and wilt slowly in a saucepan with a couple of thyme leaves and 2 tablespoons olive oil. Add 1 liter/1 quart water and stir. When it comes to the boil add the barley, salt and pepper. Cook covered for 30 minutes, but stir frequently, add the milk which must be at room temperature. As soon as it boils, remove from the stove and put the soup into individual bowls. Add a squiggle of olive oil to each, garnish with thyme leaves and serve. Barley soup, known as *tchicha* which means coarsely ground grains – can also be made with cornmeal that you pour gradually into boiling water stirring constantly, and a little tomato.

COUSCOUS

Couscous is the pride of Moroccan cuisine, the greatest gift of the rural culture, the traditional meal for Fridays – the Moroccan Sabbath. Succulent chunks of meat or fish with vegetables crown a golden dome of semolina that has soaked up the flavors during lengthy cooking. Whether it is prepared with seven vegetables or onions and raisins, hearty meat or delicate chicken, it is indeed a one-dish meal that combines the energy of grains, the nourishment of proteins and the benefits of vegetable fibers.

3

7 VEGETABLE COUSCOUS

1 kg/2 lbs medium grain
   couscous (see page 46)
800 gr/ 1 3/4 lbs lean beef
300 gr/12 oz dried chickpeas
3 potatoes
3 ripe tomatoes
2 carrots
2 onions
2 bell peppers
200 gr/8 oz white turnips (see
   note)
300 gr/13 oz (1 wedge) head-
   cabbage
350 gr/13 oz (1 wedge) peeled
   pumpkin
1 stalk celery
Powdered saffron (one sachet)
Sweet paprika
1 bunch green coriander
   and parsley tied together
Salt and pepper
80 gr/3 oz butter
Olive oil

Servings: 8	
Preparation time: 40'+ 8h	
Cooking time: 2h	
Difficulté: ●●	
Flavor: ●●	
Kcal (per serving): 815	
Proteins (per serving): 38	
Fats (per serving): 21	
Nutritional value: ●●●	

1 Before you begin, soak the chickpeas for 8 hours. Prepare the vegetables and herbs: chop the onions and celery; slice the others including 1 tomato; put the other 2 tomatoes through the food-mill. Cut the meat into stew-size chunks, brown in the bottom half of the couscous pot with the chopped onion and celery, 4 tablespoons olive oil and 1/4 of the butter.

2 After 10 minutes add the drained chickpeas, mashed tomatoes, 1 tablespoon paprika, the saffron, salt and pepper and enough hot water to cover completely, put on the lid and cook slowly for 30 minutes. In the meantime, combine the couscous with water, olive oil and salt and pepper in a large concave plate (see page 46), then put it in the top half of the couscous pot. When the 30 minutes are up, put it on top and cook slowly for 20 minutes from when it starts to steam.

3 Remove the couscous from the stove, turn it back onto the plate and stir, adding water to moisten. Let it sit for a few minutes, and add the carrots, cabbage, pump and bouquet of herbs to the meat and chickpeas; put the couscous back in the cooker and put it on top.

4 Cook for 20 minutes, and repeat the above steps for the couscous (salt to taste); while it sits add the turnips, potatoes, sliced tomatoes and peppers, plus a little hot water, if needed, to the pot with the meat. Once again season to taste with salt and pepper, put the upper part back on top and steam 20 minutes longer.
Turn the couscous onto a serving platter, dot with the remaining butter, mix and shape it into a mound, moistening with a little of the cooking liquid. Make a well in the middle and fill it with the meat, arrange the vegetables all around. Put the remaining

vegetables on another platter; strain the remaining liquid and serve it in a bowl on the side.

To cook couscous to perfection you need a couscous pot that consists of the gdra, *the bottom saucepan for slowly cooking the meat and vegetables (originally it was put on hot charcoals), and the* kskess *with a perforated bottom. The* kskess *fits tightly over the saucepan and that is where you put the couscous that gets steamed by the cooking vapors. Turnips are widely used in Moroccan foods. If you cannot find them Mohammed El Gara suggests using Japanese daikon that is available in nearly all supermarkets.*

LAMB COUSCOUS

Mix the couscous with water, olive oil, salt and pepper (see below). prepare the vegetables: chop one onion with the celery, dice the rest. Cut the meat into stew-size pieces and brown it in the bottom of the couscous pot with the celery and onion, half the butter, salt and pepper; after 10 minutes add the cabbage, enough hot water to cover and bring to the boil. Cover with the top portion of the couscous pot with the couscous. Cook over a medium flame for 20 minutes from when the steam starts to rise from the couscous. Turn the couscous onto a large plate, moisten with water, mix and let rest about 10 minutes. Add the carrots, pumpkin, diced onions, hot pepper and 1 teaspoon coriander seeds. Put the couscous back on top and steam for another 20 minutes. Remove the couscous and mix as described above, and let it rest. In the meantime add the eggplant, potatoes, tomatoes, peppers, turnips and saffron to the meat. Season to taste with salt and pepper, add a little hot water, and put the couscous back on top to steam for 20 minutes more. Turn the couscous onto a serving platter, dot with the rest of the butter and mix. Shape it into a mound and moisten with a little of the broth. Arrange the meat and vegetables in the middle and serve with any extra vegetables and the strained broth on the side.

---

1 kg/2 lbs medium grain
  couscous, see below
800 gr/ 1 3/4 lbs boned
  shoulder of lamb or mutton
3 carrots
3 tomatoes
3 onions
500 gr/1 lb head-cabbage
1 sweet eggplant
1 stalk celery
400 gr/14 oz peeled pumpkin
  (1 slice)
1 hot red pepper
Coriander seeds
1 sachet powdered saffron
Salt and pepper
100 gr/4 oz butter
Olive oil

Servings: 8	
Preparation time: 40'	
Cooking time 1h 15'	
Difficulté: ●●	
Flavor: ●●●	
Kcal (per serving): 815	
Proteins (per serving): 37	
Fats (per serving) 25	
Nutritional value: ●●●	

COUSCOUS

Couscous is made of sifted semolina and flour that are rubbed together with salted water in a large bowl (*gsàa*) and put through sieves (*ghorbal*) to get smaller and smaller even grains. In addition to medium grain couscous, the most common, there is a finer type known as *seffa*. The most widely used variety is made of hard, durum wheat, but it is also made from barley or corn (*belboula*). All our recipes, except for one on page 48, use bulk couscous that is neither precooked nor dehydrated. For convenience, here is a summary of Mohammed El Gara's suggestions on how to prepare couscous. Spread couscous on a large plate, rub with your hands, or mix with a spatula, sprinkling it with water and a little oil (2-3 tablespoons according to the quantity), salt and pepper (see page 52, step 1); then put it in the top part of the couscous pot to steam (see page 44). The meat and vegetables in the bottom portion of the couscous pot cook steadily, but the couscous itself has to be removed, mixed and moistened with cold water several times (see page 50 step 2), so that the grains separate and fluff. Always let the couscous rest for 5 minutes after mixing. When it is done, mix it for the last time with butter (or *smen*, when appropriate, see page 47) directly on the serving platter before shaping it into a mound and moistening with the cooking liquid. If, to save time and effort, you do opt for the precooked variety available in all supermarkets, follow the instructions on the package.

| 750 gr/26 oz medium grain couscous (see page 46) |
| 1.5 kg/ 3 lbs oxtail |
| 2 carrots |
| 2 tomatoes |
| 2 zucchini |
| 1 big onion |
| 1 stalk celery |
| 250 gr/8 oz turnips (see page 45) |
| 1 bunch green coriander |
| Sweet paprika |
| 45 gr/ 1 1/2 oz / 3 TBS salted butter (or *smen*) |
| Olive oil |
| Salt and pepper |

Servings: 6	
Preparation time: 40'	
Cooking time 2h	
Difficulté: ●●	
Flavor: ●●●	
Kcal (per serving): 769	
Proteins (per serving): 46	
Fats (per serving) 19	
Nutritional value: ●●	

OXTAIL COUSCOUS

Prepare all the vegetables and slice them; rinse and dry the oxtail then cut it into pieces. Brown in the bottom portion of the couscous pot with the chopped onion, 5 tablespoons olive oil, the coriander, salt and pepper and 1 teaspoon paprika. After 10 minutes add enough water to cover and bring to the boil. Cover the pot and simmer for 30 minutes, then replace the lid with the upper portion of the couscous pot containing the couscous, as described on page 46.

Cook over a medium flame for 20 minutes from when the steam comes through the couscous. Turn the couscous onto a large plate , moisten with water, mix and then let it rest for 5 minutes. Put the couscous back on the pot and steam for 20 minutes. Turn it onto the plate again, moisten mix and let it rest. Now, add the vegetables to the meat (and hot water if necessary) season to taste with salt and pepper and put the couscous back to steam for 20 minutes more.

Put the couscous onto a serving platter, dot with the butter and mix; moisten with a little of the cooking liquid and shape into a mound. Make a well in the middle and fill it with the oxtail and vegetables. Serve any extra meat and vegetables on a separate platter and the strained broth in a bowl.

Smen is clarified, salted butter that is left in a cool place for a year until it turns rancid. It is used to flavor many Moroccan dishes: the older it is the better (and it is also quite expensive). If you cannot obtain genuine smen, Mohammed El Gara suggests blending salted butter with a little cheese streaked with green mold such as Roquefort or Gorgonzola.

BELBOUA COUSCOUS

1 Before you begin, soak the chickpeas for 8 hours. Clean the vegetables, peel and cube the potatoes. Cut the meat into chunks and season with a pinch of pepper and saffron stems. Drain the chickpeas and put them into the bottom portion of the couscous pot along with the meat, the onion chopped together with the coriander and parsley, 2 tablespoons paprika and salt. Add 4 tablespoons olive oil, add enough water (about 4 liters/4 quarts) to cover and bring to the boil. Put a lid on the pot and cook slowly for 30 minutes.

2 Prepare the couscous (page 46) mixing it with water, olive oil, salt and pepper, put it into the top portion of the couscous pot and place it over the bottom. Cook for 20 minutes from when the steam starts to pass through the grains. Turn the couscous onto a large plate, mix with a little salted water and let it rest for 5 minutes. Add the carrots and turnips to the pot, put the couscous back on top and steam for another 20 minutes.

3 Put the couscous back on the plate, mix again as above and let it sit for 5 minutes. Add the potatoes, tomatoes, pumpkin and zucchini to the pot, put the couscous back on top and cook slowly for 25 minutes from when the couscous starts to steam (add some hot water as needed and season to taste with salt and pepper). Put the couscous onto the serving platter, dot with the butter and mix; shape it into a cone, make a little well in the middle and fill it with meat and vegetables, moisten with a little broth. Put the rest of the vegetables on a platter, strain the broth and serve it on the side.

1 kg/2 lbs corn or barley
    couscous (see page 46)
1 kg/ 2 lbs lean mutton
250 gr/8 oz dried chickpeas
4 carrots
4 potatoes
4 ripe tomatoes
4 zucchini
2 onions
400 gr/14 oz peeled pumpkin
    (1 slice)
300 gr/12 oz turnips
    (see page 45)
1 bunch green coriander and
    parsley
Sweet paprika and saffron
    stems
80 gr/3 oz salted butter
    (or smen, see page 47)
Olive oil

Servings: 8-10	
Preparation time: 1h40'+ 8h	
Cooking time 2h	
Difficulté: ●●	
Flavor: ●●●	
Kcal (per serving): 724	
Proteins (per serving): 42	
Fats (per serving) 11	
Nutritional value: ●●●	

If you cannot find corn or barley couscous, this just may be the perfect time to try and make the "ordinary" kind yourself, following Mohammed El Gara's instructions. Pour one cup of semolina onto a large, concave plate, take a handful and use your fingertips to rub it on your palm gradually adding salted water by the drop (the contents of a small bowl will be all the water you need) to make little, evenly sized balls. Continue working adding semolina and water until you have used up all the ingredients, and remember to add a drop of olive oil. For this dish you need large, coarse couscous grains, otherwise you have to put it through sieves several times to make them smaller. Set the couscous aside to "rest" (remember that practice makes perfect) and let's continue with the recipe.

ONION AND RAISIN COUSCOUS

1 Clean the onions; chop one and slice all the others. Cut the meat into chunks, brown the meat in the bottom portion of the couscous pot with 4 tablespoons olive oil, the chopped onion, parsley and coriander, 1 teaspoon saffron stems and salt and pepper. After five minutes add enough water to cover (about 3 liters/3 quarts) put a lid on the pot and simmer for 30 minutes.

2 Prepare the couscous (see page 46) with water, oil, salt and pepper. Put it into the top portion of the couscous pot and set it over the meat. Cook for 20 minutes from when the steam starts to come through the couscous. Turn the couscous onto a large plate, mix to aerate and moisten slightly. Let it rest for 5 minutes while the meat continues to cook uncovered. Then put it back over the meat; repeat this step twice more, letting the couscous steam for 20 minutes each time.

3 In the meantime slowly wilt the sliced onions in another pan with 6 tablespoons olive oil. When they are transparent add the sugar, salt and 1 teaspoon powdered saffron. Caramelize the onions over the lowest flame, with a lid on the pan, for about 30 minutes while the couscous is steaming. If needed add a drop or two of hot water and stir gently.

4 Add the raisins and honey, stir, cover and continue cooking as slowly as possible for another 30 minutes (so that the onions are done at the same time as the couscous), adding a little hot water as needed and stirring now and then.
Put the couscous on the serving platter, dot with the butter and mix. Make a dome with a well in the middle, fill that with the meat, cover with the caramelized onions and moisten with the cooking broth. Strain the remaining broth and serve it on the side with the extra onions and raisins.

---

1 kg/2 lbs medium grain couscous (see page 46)
1.2 kg/ 2 1/5 lbs lean beef
10 onions (about 2 kg/4 1/2 lbs)
300 gr/12 oz raisins
80 gr/3 oz sugar
15 gr/1 tablespoon honey
1 bunch green coriander and parsley, chopped
Saffron stems and powdered saffron
Salt and pepper
60 gr/ 2 oz butter
Olive oil

Servings: 8
Preparation time: 40'
Cooking time 1h 45'
Difficulté: ●●
Flavor: ●●
Kcal (per serving): 1023
Proteins (per serving): 47
Fats (per serving) 19
Nutritional value: ●●●

51

CHICKEN WITH T'FAYA COUSCOUS

1 Spread the couscous on a large, concave plate, mix by adding water, olive oil, salt and pepper. Put it into the upper portion of the couscous pot; fill the bottom portion with lots of water (about 4 liters/4 quarts). Fit the couscous on top, put the pot on the stove and bring to the boil. Steam the couscous for 20 minutes; remove from the stove, turn it back onto the concave plate, mix and moisten with a little water and let it set for 5 minutes.

750 gr /26 oz medium grain
   couscous (see page 46)
1.5 kg/3 lbs chicken ready to cook
1 onion
1 bunch green coriander and
   parsley
Ground ginger and saffron
   stems
Salt and pepper
45 g/ 1 1/2 oz/ 3 tablespoons
   butter
Olive oil

For the t'faya
4 onions
200 gr/8 oz raisins
50 gr/ 1 1/2 oz/ 3 tablespoons
   sugar
Ground cinnamon
Orange flower oil
30 gr/1 oz / 1 tablespoon
   butter
Pepper

Servings: 6	
Preparation time: 40'	
Cooking time 1h 15'	
Difficulté: ●●	
Flavor: ●●	
Kcal (per serving): 1077	
Proteins (per serving): 40	
Fats (per serving) 37	
Nutritional value: ●●●	

2 In the meantime, cut the chicken into about 20 pieces. Chop one onion and in a bowl combine it with the chopped coriander and parsley, 1 teaspoon ginger, a pinch of saffron stems, salt and pepper and 1 tablespoon olive oil. Mix.

3 Discard the water in the bottom of the couscous pot; dry it well. Brown the chicken in 2 tablespoons olive oil, turning the pieces to they are evenly cooked. Add the seasoning you prepared in step 2, a little water and stir. Put the couscous back on top, steam for 20 minutes and repeat the procedure in step 1. Steam the couscous for another 20 minutes – check the chicken and add hot water if necessary.

4 While the chicken and couscous are cooking prepare the *t'faya*. Slice the 3 remaining onions and wilt in a saucepan with 3 tablespoons olive oil, add the raisins, 1 teaspoon cinnamon, the butter and a dash of pepper, stir and add enough water to just cover. Bring to the boil and simmer for 30 minutes, after about 15 minutes add 1 teaspoon orange flower oil. When the cooking time is almost up, add the sugar, and stir so that it dissolves slowly. Turn the couscous onto the serving platter, dot with butter and mix; shape it into a dome with a well in the middle. Fill the well with the chicken topped with the *t'faya* and moisten with a little of the cooking liquid. Strain the rest of the liquid and serve it on the side with any extra *t'faya*.

TROTTER AND FAVA BEAN COUSCOUS

750 gr/26 oz medium grain couscous (see page 46)
1 kg/2 lbs beef trotter
450 gr/ 1 lb dried, shelled fava beans
1 big onion
1 bunch green coriander and parsley, tied together (plus parsley for garnish)
Saffron stems
Powdered saffron (1 sachet) and ground ginger
Salt and pepper
50 gr/ 1 1/2 oz/ 3 tablespoons salted butter (or *smen*, see page 47)
Olive oil

Servings: 6	
Preparation time: 40'+6h	
Cooking time 1h45'	
Difficulté: ●●	
Flavor: ●●●	
Kcal (per serving): 902	
Proteins (per serving): 54	
Fats (per serving) 21	
Nutritional value: ●●●	

1 This recipe calls for dried fava beans, that you must soak for at least 6 hours, When they are in season you can use fresh beans, and will need 1 kg/ 2 lbs, shelled. Clean and chop the onion, and wilt it slowly in 4 tablespoons olive oil in the bottom portion of the couscous pot.

2 Clean, Rinse, dry and cut the trotter into chunks, after 5 minutes add the it to the pot, cook slowly turning the pieces so that they brown evenly.

3 After 10 minutes add the bouquet of coriander and parsley, the powdered saffron and a pinch of saffron stems, 1 teaspoon ginger, salt and pepper and 2 liters/2 quarts water. Bring to a gentle boil and cook covered for 30 minutes. In the meantime prepare the couscous (see page 46) by mixing it with water, olive oil, salt and pepper in a large, concave plate.

4 Put the couscous into the upper portion of the couscous pot, and place that on top of the pot with the meat. Cook for 20 minutes from when it starts to steam. Turn the couscous onto the plate, mix and moisten and let it sit for 5 minutes. Put it back into the pot and steam for 20 minutes more. Turn the couscous back onto the plate. Put the drained fava beans into the pot with the meat and stir. Mix and moisten the couscous and once again, let it rest for 5 minutes and then steam for another 20 minutes. Check the liquid in the pot and add hot water if needed. Put the couscous on a serving platter, dot

with butter and mix. Shape it into a dome, moisten with the cooking liquid, make a well in the middle and fill it with the meat and beans. Discard the bouquet of herbs, garnish with fresh parsley and serve the strained broth on the side.

FISH COUSCOUS

750 gr/26 oz medium grain
   couscous (see page 46)
1.5 kg/3 lbs assorted white fish
   (gray mullet, angler, sea
   bream, etc.)
1 carrot
1 onion
1 stalk celery
1 zucchini
2 ripe tomatoes
1/2 head-cabbage
200 gr/8 oz turnips
   (see page 45)
Saffron stems
Crushed coriander seeds
Ground hot red pepper and
   Cumin (on the side)
Salt and pepper
40 gr/ 1 1/2 oz/ 2 3/4 table
   spoons butter (or smen,
   see page 47)
Olive oil

Servings: 6	
Preparation time: 40'	
Cooking time 1h35'	
Difficulté: ●●	
Flavor: ●●●	
Kcal (per serving): 912	
Proteins (per serving): 52	
Fats (per serving) 31	
Nutritional value: ●●●	

When you clean and gut the fish, keep the heads, tails and other parts for the broth as well as the vegetable scraps. Put all the scraps into a pot, add 2 liters/2 quarts water, a pinch each of pepper and hot red pepper. Simmer uncovered for 30 minutes, skimming frequently. Then strain the broth. Chop the onion and wilt it slowly in the bottom portion of the couscous pot with 3 tablespoons olive oil. After 5 minutes add the broth plus enough hot water to make up for the liquid that evaporated, the cut up cabbage, carrot and celery, a pinch each of saffron stems and coriander seeds. Cover and bring to the boil. In the meantime, prepare the couscous, by mixing it with water, olive oil, salt and pepper (see page 46). Put the couscous in the upper portion of the couscous pot, fit it over the bottom and cook for 20 minutes from when it starts to steam. Turn the couscous onto a concave plate, mix and moisten and let it sit for 5 minutes. Put it back in the pot, add the cut tomatoes, turnips and zucchini to the vegetables, along with a pinch of cumin and add salt to taste. Put the couscous on top and steam for 20 minutes. Once again, mix and moisten the couscous, add the fish pieces to the vegetables, season to taste with salt and pepper and steam for 10-12 minutes. Turn the couscous onto the serving platter, dot with butter and mix. Shape it into a dome with a well in the middle; fill the cavity with the fish and vegetables and moisten with the broth. Strain the rest of the broth and serve it on the side; and prepare a small bowl with ground hot pepper as an optional seasoning.

TAJINES

One of Morocco's most famous traditional specialties tajine (also spelled tahine or tadjine) gets its name from the glazed earthenware pot used to prepare it, the tajine slaoui. It consists of a saucepan with a tall, often nicely decorated, very tight-fitting, cone-shaped lid that transforms it into a sort of Dutch oven.
The high "hat" lets steam circulate, making it the ideal vessel for cooking stews. Here is a series of tasty fish and meat recipes made with this "magic pot."
It was created to be used on hot coals on the hearth, on a stovetop Mohammed El Gara strongly recommends a wire mesh screen to "scatter" the flame, otherwise there is the risk of the pot cracking.
If you do not have a tajine, you can use a pot with a tight-fitting lid or a pressure cooker and make the necessary time adjustments. For the lucky ones who do have a tajine – they are available in specialty stores everywhere – remember to bring it to the table with the lid on to unleash the wonderful aromas all at once.

4

MUSSEL TAJINE

2.5 kg/ 5 lbs mussels
(also for garnish)
3 ripe tomatoes
3 cloves garlic
1 nice bunch green coriander
and parsley
Ground cumin
Salted lemon rind (for garnish)
Salt and pepper
Olive oil

Servings:	6
Preparation time:	25'
Cooking time:	15'
Difficulty:	●
Flavor:	●●
Kcal (per serving):	211
Proteins (per serving):	17
Fats (per serving):	13
Nutritional value:	●

Prepare the tomatoes and herbs. Scrape the mussels, rinse them under cold running water. Put them in a skillet with a little water and cook quickly over a lively flame to open. Shell about four fifths, leaving the rest on the shell. Strain the cooking liquid. Chop the garlic and wilt it slowly in the *tajine* with 3 tablespoons olive oil; add the cubed tomatoes, cook slowly and stir to blend the flavors. After 10 minutes add the shelled mussels and broth, season to taste with salt and pepper. Cover the *tajine* and cook slowly for 10 minutes. When it is almost done, add the mussels in the shells and a pinch of cumin; sprinkle with chopped coriander and parsley and garnish with the salted lemon rind. Close the *tajine* and bring it to the table to delight your guests.

GURNARD TAJINE

Clean and gut the fish; discard the head and fins, and cut it into slices. Prepare the chermoula: squeeze the lemon; peel the garlic and crush it to a paste, in a bowl combine it with the lemon juice, finely chopped coriander and parsley, salt, pepper 1 teaspoon each of cumin and paprika, the crumbled cinnamon stick and 2 tablespoons olive oil. Mix well and add the fish slices. Cover the bowl and refrigerate for 1 hour, turning the slices now and then.

Peel and slice the potatoes; clean the peppers removing the seeds, stem and rib and cut them into strips. Clean the tomatoes and cut round slices. Wash the half lemon and slice that too. Put 2 tablespoons olive oil in the *tajine*, line the bottom with the potato circles and brown briefly.

After 5 minutes add the fish, peppers, lemon slices and half the chermoula diluted with a glass of water. Cover the *tajine* and cook as slowly as possible for 15 minutes. Remove the lid, add the tomatoes, the other half of the chermoula, season with salt and pepper, cover and cook 10 minutes more. Open the *tajine* at the table.

Chermoula is a spicy, aromatic marinade. Its ingredients vary according to the recipe – usually seafoods, but also grilled or tajine-stewed meats – and local or family traditions. Its important role in Moroccan cooking is evident from the many times you will come across it in these recipes selected by Mohammed El Gara.

1.2 kg/ 2 1/2 lbs gurnard
600 gr/1 1/2 lbs potatoes
1/2 red and 1/2 green pepper
  (200 gr/8 oz total)
3 tomatoes
1/2 lemon
Salt and pepper
Olive oil

For the chermoula:
1 bunch green coriander
  and parsley
3 cloves garlic
1 lemon
ground cumin and sweet
  paprika
1 stick cinnamon
Salt and pepper
Olive oil

Servings: 4

Preparation time: 20 + 1h'

Cooking time: 30'

Difficulty: ●●

Flavor: ●●●

Kcal (per serving): 816

Proteins (per serving): 43

Fats (per serving): 54

Nutritional value: ●●

PRAWN TAJINE

12 prawns or jumbo shrimp
800 gr/ 1 3/4 lbs potatoes
5 ripe tomatoes
1 big onion
4 cloves garlic
1 bunch green coriander and
  parsley (also for garnish)
Saffron stems
Sweet paprika
1 piece salted lemon rind
Small black olives (about 20
  for garnish)
Salt and pepper
Olive oil

Servings: 4	
Preparation time: 25'	
Cooking time: 25'	
Difficulty:	●●
Flavor:	●●
Kcal (per serving):	372
Proteins (per serving):	19
Fats (per serving):	11
Nutritional value:	●●

1 Clean the prawns, remove the shells and heads; rinse and pat them dry. Clean the tomatoes, remove the seeds and reduce them to pulp in the blender or food mill. Save the liquid (or use an equivalent amount of tomato purée). Peel and dice the potatoes.

2 Clean the onion and garlic and chop finely together with the coriander and parsley. Wilt the mixture slowly in the *tajine* with 3 tablespoons olive oil, 1 teaspoon paprika and a pinch each of saffron stems, salt and pepper.

3 Add the potatoes and the puréed tomatoes along with the liquid (if necessary add a little hot water), stir. Cover the *tajine* and cook slowly for 15 minutes.

4 Add the prawns and grated lemon rind, cover and cook 6 minutes more. Garnish with chopped parsley and pitted olives. Put the lid back on the *tajine* and serve. Rice is an alternative to the potatoes if you like.

EEL TAJINE

1.5 kg/ 3 lbs conger eel
(or moray eel or white fish
to slice)
2 onions
200 gr/8 oz raisins
2 sticks cinnamon
Parsley and 1 lemon
(for garnish)
Salt and pepper
Olive oil

For the chermoula:
1 bunch green coriander
and parsley
2 cloves garlic
Sweet paprika
Ground cinnamon
Powdered saffron (1 sachet)
1 strip lemon rind
Salt and pepper
Olive oil

Servings: 6	
Preparation time: 25'+ 1h	
Cooking time: 40'	
Difficulty: ●	
Flavor: ●●●	
Kcal (per serving): 505	
Proteins (per serving): 48	
Fats (per serving): 22	
Nutritional value: ●●	

Prepare the onion, garlic and herbs; clean and gut the eel, discard the head and tails, rinse it and slice it. In a bowl combine a chopped mixture of coriander, parsley, garlic and lemon rind with 1/2 tablespoon paprika, 1 teaspoon each cinnamon, saffron, salt, pepper, and 5 tablespoons olive oil. Set aside

Put the *chermoula* in a deep platter with the eel slices on top, cover and refrigerate for 1 hour, turning the eel occasionally.

Chop the onions and wilt slowly in the *tajine* with 4 tablespoons olive oil; after 5 minutes add the raisins and cinnamon sticks; add 2 ladles of hot water, cover and cook slowly for 15 minutes.

Add the eel slices, dilute the *chermoula* with hot water and pour over the eel. Season to taste with salt and pepper, cover and cook over as low as flame as possible for 15, maximum 20 minutes. Sprinkle with chopped parsley, garnish with lemon slices. Put the lid back on and open the *tajine* at the table.

SARDINE TAJINE

1 kg/2 lbs fresh sardines	
100 gr/4 oz rice for timbales	
5 big ripe tomatoes	
5 cloves garlic	
1 bunch green coriander and parsley (also for garnish)	
1 stick cinnamon	
Sweet paprika and cumin	
1/2 lemon	
Salted lemon rind (for garnish)	
Flour	
Salt and pepper	
Olive oil	

Servings: 4	
Preparation time: 30'	
Cooking time: 35'	
Difficulty: ●●	
Flavor: ●●●	
Kcal (per serving): 443	
Proteins (per serving): 33	
Fats (per serving): 21	
Nutritional value: ●●	

Prepare the vegetables and herbs; squeeze the half lemon. Boil the rice for 10 minutes, drain and set aside. Clean the sardines, discarding the heads and backbones, rinse and pat dry. Put them through the blender with the rice, 3 cloves garlic, coriander and parsley, 1/2 teaspoon cumin, 1/2 tablespoons paprika, 3 tablespoons olive oil, salt and pepper. Cover your hands with flour, and start making walnut-size balls with the rice and fish mixture (to help them keep their shape, blend in a little flour and egg white if necessary). Crush the rest of the garlic and wilt it in the *tajine* with 3 tablespoons olive oil, add cinnamon, salt and pepper add 1/2 glass water and then the tomatoes cut in pieces. Bring to the boil, put the lid on the *tajine* and cook for 15 minutes. Add the sardine and rice balls, cover and simmer slowly 15 minutes more. Add the lemon juice, and bring the *tajine* to the table with the lid on.

Gilthead Tajine

1.2 kg/1 1/2 lbs gilthead or
   other white fish
2 onions
2 potatoes
2 ripe tomatoes
1 carrot
Parsley and 1 lemon
   (for garnish)
Salt and pepper
Olive oil

For the chermoula:
1 bunch green coriander
3 cloves garlic
Ground cumin and sweet
   paprika
1 lemon
Salt
Olive oil

Servings:	4
Preparation time:	30'+ 1h
Cooking time:	30'
Difficulty:	●●
Flavor:	●●●
Kcal (per serving):	617
Proteins (per serving):	48
Fats (per serving):	33
Nutritional value:	●●

1 First prepare the *chermoula:* squeeze the lemon, wash the coriander and crush it in a mortar (or put it through the blender) with the peeled garlic and a pinch of salt. Put the paste on a tray, add 2 tablespoons paprika, 1 of cumin, the lemon juice and 2 tablespoons olive oil, mix and let rest.

2 Clean and gut the fish, discard the head, tail, fins and backbone, fillet it (this is not so easy, so it may be best to have your fish vendor do it!), and place it on the tray with the *chermoula.* Cover and refrigerate for 1 hour, turning the slices occasionally.

3 Clean the vegetables; slice the onion and potatoes in circles, julienne the carrots, cube the tomatoes. Pour 3 tablespoons olive oil into the *tajine,* line the bottom with alternating layers of onion and potato slices, cover and stew slowly for 15 minutes.

4 Remove the *tajine* from the stove, add the fish filets, season each fillet with 1/2 tablespoon oil and add the marinade. Scatter the carrots and tomatoes over the fish, season to taste with salt and pepper, cover and cook as slowly as possible for 15 minutes. Sprinkle with chopped parsley and thin lemon wedges. Put the lid back on and bring the *tajine* to the table. When in season, you can use fresh fava beans and artichokes instead of potatoes and onions: Mohammed El Gara assures that it is just as delicious!

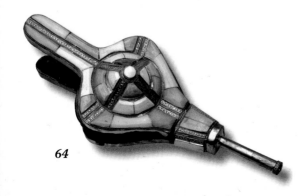

1

2

ANGLER TAJINE

1 Prepare the *chermoula:* squeeze the lemons. Clean the other ingredients, finely chop the garlic with the coriander, parsley and salted lemon. Put the mixture into a bowl big and deep enough to hold the fish medallions, add 1 teaspoon paprika and a pinch each of cumin and saffron stems, salt and pepper, the lemon juice and 2 tablespoons olive oil. Mix.

2 Add the fish medallions, cover and refrigerate for 1 hour, turning now and then. In the meantime pit the olives and cut them into circles.

3 Grease the bottom of the *tajine* with olive oil, arrange the fish inside and cover with the marinade.

4 Add the rest of the marinade, put the lid on the *tajine* and cook over a low flame for 15 minutes.

5 Add the olives, season to taste with salt and pepper, cover the *tajine* and cook for another 5 minutes. Sprinkle with chopped parsley and decorate with lemon circles.

1.5 kg/3 lbs angler (monkfish), sliced
300 gr/12 oz green and black olives
Parsley and 1 lemon (for garnish)
Salt and pepper
For the chermoula:
2 lemons
3 cloves garlic
1 bunch green coriander and parsley
1 wedge salted lemon
Ground cumin, sweet paprika and saffron stems
Salt and pepper
Olive oil

Servings: 6	
Preparation time: 20'+ 1h	
Cooking time: 20'	
Difficulty: ●●	
Flavor: ●●●	
Kcal (per serving): 316	
Proteins (per serving): 38	
Fats (per serving): 17	
Nutritional value: ●●	

LAMB AND ARTICHOKE TAJINE

800 gr/ 1 3/4 lbs lean lamb
6 artichokes (about 1.2 kg/ 2 1/2 lbs)
12 black olives
1/2 lemon
Parsley (for garnish)
Ground ginger
Powdered saffron (one sachet)
Salt and pepper
Olive oil

Servings:	4
Preparation time:	20'
Cooking time:	1h
Difficulty:	●●
Flavor:	●●
Kcal (per serving):	412
Proteins (per serving):	48
Fats (per serving):	14
Nutritional value:	●●●

Squeeze the lemon (save a piece of the rind); clean the artichokes discarding stems and tough outer leaves, slice and put into a bowl of water and the lemon juice. Cut the meat into stew-size pieces. Put it into the *tajine* with a pinch of salt and pepper, 1 teaspoon ginger, the saffron, 3 tablespoons olive oil and 3 ladles of water; cover and cook slowly for 1 hour. During the last ten minutes, uncover the pot, add the drained artichokes, the pitted olives and the lemon peel cut into matchstick-thin slices; season to taste with salt and pepper and add more hot water if needed. Finish cooking, garnish with parsley, close the *tajine* and bring it to the table.

LIVER AND LIGHTS TAJINE

Clean the livers and lights and cut into pieces; clean and dice the tomatoes. Chop the onion and garlic together and wilt slowly in the *tajine* with 4 tablespoons olive oil. Add the meat pieces and brown slowly for 10 minutes: season with salt and pepper, 1 tablespoon paprika and 1 teaspoon turmeric then add the tomatoes. Put the lid on the *tajine* and cook over a moderate flame for 1 hour, adding hot water if it tends to dry. During the last 10 minutes of cooking time, add 1 teaspoon cumin, a dash of hot pepper and the olives, cook uncovered to reduce the sauce. Put the lid back on and bring the *tajine* to the table, serve with salted lemon slices on the side if you like.

900 gr/2 lbs two complete lamb livers and lights (heart, liver, lungs, trachea)
4 ripe tomatoes
300 gr/12 oz green olives (pitted)
1 onion
4 cloves garlic
Ground cumin, turmeric, sweet paprika and hot pepper)
1 salted lemon (optional)
Salt and pepper
Olive oil

Servings: 6
Preparation time: 20'
Cooking time: 1h 10'
Difficulty: ●●
Flavor: ●●●
Kcal (per serving): 282
Proteins (per serving): 25
Fats (per serving): 17
Nutritional value: ●●

MUTTON TAJINE

1.5 kg/ 3 lbs leg or shoulder of mutton, on the bone
5 onions
300 gr/12 oz shelled, blanched almonds
200 gr/8 oz raisins
Sweet paprika and saffron stems
50 gr / 1 1/2 oz/ 3 tablespoons Sugar
Confectioners' sugar and cinnamon (optional for garnish)
Salt and pepper
Olive oil

Servings:	6
Preparation time:	25'
Cooking time:	1h 20'
Difficulty:	●●
Flavor:	●●●
Kcal (per serving):	428
Proteins (per serving):	43
Fats (per serving):	12
Nutritional value:	●●

1 Toast the almonds in a dry, non-stick pan, cut them into lengthwise slivers. Clean the onions: slice one thinly and crush the others to a pulp in a mortar or in the blender.

2 Cut the meat into even pieces, arrange them in the *tajine* with the sliced onion and almonds, season with 1 tablespoon paprika, a pinch of saffron stems, the sugar, salt and pepper. Pour on about 1 cup water, cover and cook over a low flame for 1 hour.

3 Remove the meat from the *tajine*, set it aside and keep it warm. Put the mashed onions into the pot with 3 tablespoons olive oil, stir, cover and cook slowly for 20 minutes.

4 Add the raisins to the sauce, cook uncovered and stir for 5 minutes, put the meat back into the pot to reheat (check the seasoning) and serve drenched in the sauce that should be quite thick. Tradition says that this dish should be sprinkled with cinnamon and confectioners' sugar, but it is fine without!

CHICKEN TAJINE

1.2 kg/2 1/2 lbs chicken,
  ready to cook
2 eggs
1 onion
1 clove garlic
1 bunch green coriander
  (also for garnish)
1 bunch parsley
1 lemon
2 sticks cinnamon
Ground ginger, sweet paprika
  powdered saffron and saffron
  stems
Salted lemon rind (for garnish)
Salt and pepper
Olive oil

Servings: 4	
Preparation time: 20'	
Cooking time: 50'	
Difficulty: ●●	
Flavor: ●●●	
Kcal (per serving): 690	
Proteins (per serving): 44	
Fats (per serving): 53	
Nutritional value: ●●●	

1 Cut the chicken into 10-12 pieces. Clean the garlic, onion, coriander and parsley and chop them separately. Wilt the onion in the *tajine* with 3 tablespoons olive oil for 5 minutes.

2 Add the chicken pieces and brown evenly. After 10 minutes add the garlic, coriander, half the parsley, salt and pepper, stir and let the flavors combine.

3 Squeeze the lemon. Add the cinnamon, 1 level tablespoon paprika, a pinch each of powdered saffron and saffron stems and the lemon juice to the pot with the chicken. Cover and cook over as low a flame as possible for 30 minutes, adding a little hot water if it tends to dry.

4 Break the eggs in a bowl and beat with the rest of the chopped parsley, add to the chicken, stir and thicken for 5 minutes (if you prefer a creamier sauce, remove the pot from stove when you add the egg mixture and cover for 5 minutes). Season to taste with salt and pepper and serve the chicken hot with springs of coriander and sliced lemon rind on top.

Meatball Tajine

1 kg/2 lbs lean, chopped beef
3 big onions
2 lemons (1 for garnish)
1 egg white
1 bunch coriander and 1 bunch
   parsley (also for garnish)
30 gr/1 oz flour
Ground cumin, ginger and
   paprika
Saffron stems
Salt and pepper
Olive oil

Servings: 6	
Preparation time: 30'	
Cooking time: 50'	
Difficulty: ●●	
Flavor: ●●●	
Kcal (per serving): 351	
Proteins (per serving): 51	
Fats (per serving): 12	
Nutritional value: ●●	

1 Clean and chop the coriander and parsley; squeeze 1 lemon. Clean the onions: slice 2 and chop the other very finely (or put it through the blender). In a bowl, combine the meat, chopped onion and egg white with a little chopped coriander, teaspoon paprika, 1/2 teaspoon cumin, salt and pepper. Make little meatballs and roll them in the flour to coat. Set aside.

2 Pour 4 tablespoons olive oil in the *tajine*, slowly wilt the 2 sliced onions; after 5 minutes add 1 teaspoon paprika, a few saffron stems, a pinch each of salt, cumin and ginger. Add enough hot water to cover, stir, put on the lid and simmer for 15 minutes.

3 Add the meatballs with the rest of the chopped parsley and coriander, cover and cook slowly for 30 minutes.

4 When the meatballs are done, add the lemon juice and cook uncovered to reduce the sauce a little. Serve the hot meatballs decorated with parsley sprigs and lemon slices.

Beef and Olive Tajine

1.2 kg/2 1/2 lbs lean beef
400 gr/14 oz green and black
  pitted olives
1 big onion
1 tomato
6 cloves garlic
1 bunch green coriander and
  parsley
Ground ginger and saffron
Salted lemon rind (for garnish)
Salt and pepper
Olive oil

Servings: 8	
Preparation time: 20'	
Cooking time: 1h	
Difficulty: ●●	
Flavor: ●●●	
Kcal (per serving): 284	
Proteins (per serving): 31	
Fats (per serving): 16	
Nutritional value: ●●	

1 Clean and chop the onion; peel the garlic and crush in a mortar. Cut the meat into bite-size pieces, brown in the *tajine* with 5 tablespoons olive oil, 1/2 teaspoon saffron and 1 teaspoon each ginger, salt and pepper.

2 When the meat is nicely browned (about 10 minutes) add the chopped onion and mashed garlic.

3 Stir, add enough hot water to cover and put the lid on the *tajine;* simmer slowly for 35 minutes.

4 In the meantime, clean and dice the tomato. Slice the olives into circles and add them to the meat along with the tomato and chopped parsley and coriander. Put the lid back on, cook 15 minutes more and serve with thin slices of salted lemon rind.

TROTTER TAJINE

1 beef trotter, about 1 kg/2 lbs
300 gr/12 oz dried chickpeas
2 onions
2 cloves garlic
100 gr/4 oz turnips
  (see page 45)
2 sticks cinnamon
Ground ginger and sweet
  paprika
Saffron stems
Salted lemon rind (for garnish)
Salt and pepper
Olive oil

Servings: 4	
Preparation time: 20'+ 8h	
Cooking time: 1h 30'	
Difficulty: ●●	
Flavor: ●●●	
Kcal (per serving): 320	
Proteins (per serving): 46	
Fats (per serving): 12	
Nutritional value: ●●	

Soak the chickpeas for at least 8 hours before you begin. Drain and boil them for 30 minutes. In the meantime, prepare the vegetables and herbs, clean the trotter, rinse, dry and then cut it into pieces. Brown the meat in the *tajine* with 4 tablespoons olive oil, then add the chopped garlic and onions, the cinnamon sticks, 1 tablespoon paprika, 1 pinch of saffron stems, 1 teaspoon each ginger, salt and pepper. Let the flavors saturate, then add the drained chickpeas, the diced turnips, and enough water to cover it all.

Put the lid on the *tajine*, and simmer for 1 hour, uncover for the last 10 minutes of cooking time to thicken the sauce.

Serve hot with strips of salted lemon rind.

FISH

Morocco's ports on the Mediterranean and generous
Atlantic teem with fishing boats that haul in
wonderful catches. There is a bounty of sea bass,
gray mullet, gilthead and sea bream, an enormous
quantity of excellent anchovies, swordfish, mackerel
and tuna plus the exquisite silvery sardines that
sparkle on the wharves of Agadir. And there are
mussels, shrimp, lobster, crawfish, squid, cuttlefish,
sea urchins and even oysters. Moroccan cuisine
boasts an outstanding range of fish and seafood
recipes and in this chapter Mohammed El Gara
offers more to complement those in the preceding
sections of the book.

5

BAKED BASS

1 bass (or other white
  Mediterranean fish),
  1.2 kg/ 2 1/2 lbs
2 ripe tomatoes
1 bell pepper
Ground ginger
Saffron (one sachet)
Olive oil
Black olives and 1 lemon (for
  garnish)

For the chermoula:
2 cloves garlic
Cumin, paprika
1 bunch fresh coriander
Olive oil
Hot red pepper
Salt and pepper

Servings: 4	
Preparation time: 30'+2h	
Cooking time: 30'/40'+30'	
Difficulty: ●●	
Flavor: ●●	
Kcal (per serving): 492	
Proteins (per serving): 36	
Fats (per serving): 33	
Nutritional value: ●●	

1 To prepare the *chermoula,* combine the chopped coriander with the crushed garlic, 2 tablespoons olive oil, 1 tablespoon cumin, 2 tablespoons paprika, the hot red pepper and 1/2 glass water. Gut, scale and rinse the fish and then cut it into pieces.

2 Take 1 tablespoon *chermoula* and blend in 6 tablespoons olive oil, the saffron and I teaspoon ginger. Marinate the fish in the rest of the *chermoula* for 2 hours.

3 Roast the pepper in the oven, remove the skin and cut it into narrow strips. Place the strips in a greased oven dish.

4 Put the fish on top of the pepper slices along with the tomatoes cut into chunks, the *chermoula* you used for the marinade and the rest that you blended with the olive oil. Cover with a sheet of aluminum foil and bake at 160°C/325°F for 45 minutes. Serve with olives and lemon wedges.

STUFFED BASS

1 bass, ready for use
  2 kg/4 1/2 lbs
1 onion
1 potato
1 ripe tomato
1 bell pepper
1 lemon
Olive oil

For the chermoula:
6 cloves garlic
1 lemon
1 bunch green coriander and
  parsley
Ground cumin and sweet
  paprika
Salt and pepper
Olive oil

For the stuffing:
100 gr/4 oz rice for stuffing
  or timbales
100 gr/4 oz baby squid
80 gr/3 oz shrimp (just the tails)
10 green olives (pitted)
1 clove garlic
1 piece salted lemon rind
Salt and pepper

Servings: 6-8	
Preparation time: 25'+ 2h	
Cooking time: 40'	
Difficulty: ● ● ●	
Flavor: ● ● ●	
Kcal (per serving): 319	
Proteins (per serving): 26	
Fats (per serving): 16	
Nutritional value: ● ●	

1 Prepare the vegetables and herbs for use (peel and wash the potatoes); squeeze the lemon. To make the *chermoula:* crush the peeled garlic in a mortar (or put it through the blender) with the coriander, parsley, a pinch of cumin, 1 tablespoon paprika, salt and pepper. Put the paste into a bowl, add 1 tablespoon olive oil and the lemon juice, mix and set aside.

2 Clean, gut and scale the fish, trim the fins and tail, rinse it and pat it dry. Open it flat by lengthening and deepening the cut, remove the backbone by cutting the ends, but do not separate the two halves of the fish. Lay the open fish on a platter with the *chermoula,* cover and refrigerate for 2 hours.

3 Boil the rice for 10 minutes and drain. Clean the baby squid, and cut them into rings. In a bowl, combine the rice, squid, shrimp and the olives chopped together with the garlic and lemon rind, season with salt and pepper. Heat the oven to 180°C/350°F, with the fan on if possible.

4 Fill the fish with the stuffing and close with toothpicks or sew with kitchen thread. Grease an oven dish, and make a layer of potato and onion slices, put the fish on top and cover it with the sliced tomato, pepper and lemon (if you have extra stuffing, spread it around the fish). Dilute the *chermoula* with a little water and pour it over the fish, add a squiggle of olive oil and bake for 40 minutes. Serve the bass with the vegetables and open the fish at the table.

1

2

STUFFED SQUID

1.3 kg/ 2 3/4 lbs medium squid
250 gr/8 oz rice for stuffing
6 cloves garlic
1 bunch green coriander (also
  for garnish) and parsley
1 piece salted lemon rind
Ground cumin and sweet
  paprika
1 lemon (for garnish)
Salt and pepper
Olive oil

Servings: 4	
Preparation time: 30'	
Cooking time: 40'	
Difficulty: ●●●	
Flavor: ●●	
Kcal (per serving): 490	
Proteins (per serving): 36	
Fats (per serving): 15	
Nutritional value: ●●	

1 Clean and gut the squid, rinse under running water and dry, and cut off the tentacles. Boil the rice for 10 minutes. While the rice is cooking finely chop the tentacles together with 2 cloves garlic, half the coriander and parsley and the salted lemon rind.

2 Drain the rice into a saucepan, add the chopped mixture, a pinch of cumin, 1 tablespoon paprika, salt and pepper and 2 tablespoons olive oil. Let the flavors combine, cooking slowly and stirring for about 10 minutes.

3 Arrange the squid on your work table, fill the sacs with the rice mixture and close with toothpicks. Chop the rest of the garlic and remaining parsley and coriander, wilt the mixture in a big saucepan with 3 tablespoons olive oil.

4 Add the squid and 2 ladles of boiling water, cover and cook over a moderate flame for 15, maximum 20 minutes from when it reaches the boil. Only add more hot water if necessary (you can also cook it in a *tajine*). Season to taste with salt and pepper and serve garnished with lemon wedges and coriander leaves. There is a variation to this recipe with meat stuffing.

STUFFED GILTHEAD

1 Toast the almonds in a dry, non-stick pan. Boil the rice for 10 minutes then drain (you can use couscous instead, if you prefer). While the rice is cooking, clean, gut and scale the fish, trim the fins and tail, rinse it and pat it dry and open it flat. Rinse and pit the dates. Set aside about 10 dates, and chop the rest together with 60 gr/2 oz almonds. In a bowl combine the chopped mixture with the rice, sugar, a pinch each of sesame seeds, ginger, cinnamon, salt and pepper and 1 level tablespoon olive oil.

2 Use most of the mixture to stuff the fish and close it with toothpicks or sew with kitchen thread if needed; stuff the whole dates with the rest of the mixture.

3 Clean the half onion and slice it thinly, wilt with 3 tablespoons olive oil, 1 tablespoon paprika, salt and pepper in a big, low pan that can go into the oven. Put the fish on top, add the stuffed dates and 1 ladle of hot water; cover, bring to the boil and cook slowly for 20 minutes (you can use a *tajine*).

4 In the meantime, heat the oven to 200°C/400°F. When the 20 minutes are up, sprinkle the rest of the slivered almonds over the fish, bake uncovered for 10 to 15 minutes and serve immediately.

---

1 gilthead, 1 kg/2 lbs
250 gr/8 oz dates
100 gr/4 oz shelled, blanched
  almonds
80 gr/3 oz rice for stuffing
1/2 onion
5 gr/ 1 teaspoon sugar
Ground cinnamon, ginger
  and sweet paprika
Sesame seeds
Salt and pepper
Olive oil

Servings: 4	
Preparation time: 30'	
Cooking time: 35'	
Difficulty: ●●●	
Flavor: ●●●	
Kcal (per serving): 617	
Proteins (per serving): 43	
Fats (per serving): 26	
Nutritional value: ●●●	

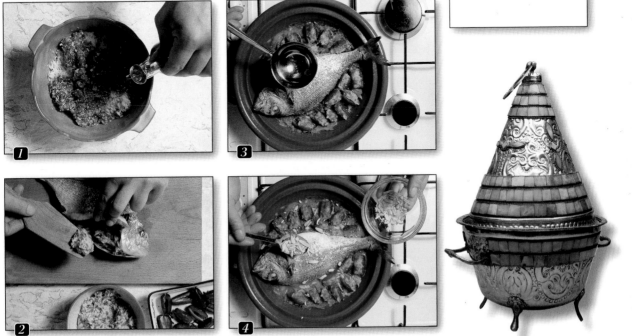

1.5 kg/3 lbs assorted, small
    fish for frying
100 gr/4 oz flour
Salt
Oil for frying

For the chermoula:
6 cloves garlic
1 bunch green coriander
    and parsley
Ground turmeric, sweet
    paprika and hot pepper
2 lemons
Salt and pepper
Olive oil

For the warm dip:
3 ripe tomatoes
1/2 onion
4 cloves garlic
1 bunch green coriander
    and parsley
Ground cumin
Tomato concentrate
Salt and pepper
Olive oil

Servings: 6	
Preparation time: 40'	
Cooking time: 1h	
Difficulty: ●●	
Flavor: ●●●	
Kcal (per serving): 489	
Proteins (per serving): 33	
Fats (per serving): 29	
Nutritional value: ●●●	

MOROCCAN FISH FRY

Prepare the herbs and vegetables for both sauces. To make the *chermoula:* squeeze the lemons into a bowl, finely chop the garlic with the parsley and coriander, add it to the lemon juice with a pinch each of turmeric and hot pepper, 1/2 tablespoon paprika, salt, pepper and 1/2 glass olive oil. Mix to emulsify and set aside.

Now for the warm dip: chop the garlic and onion with the parsley and coriander, wilt the mixture slowly in a skillet with 2 tablespoons olive oil; add the diced tomatoes and cook gently for 5 minutes. Dilute 1 tablespoon tomato concentrate in a glass of hot water and pour into the skillet. Cook over a lively flame for 20 minutes stirring constantly, 5 minutes before the cooking time is up add a pinch of cumin. Remove from the stove and keep the sauce warm.

Clean the fish (if they are small, it is sufficient to rinse and dry them, if they are big you will have to gut and scale them as well). Dredge in flour and fry a few at a time in lots of hot oil; remove with a slotted spoon when golden, drain on paper towels and sprinkle lightly with salt. Serve the crispy fish with the hot and cold sauces on the side as dips.

SWORDFISH WITH TOMATOES

Clean and finely chop the onion, sauté it in a skillet with 4 tablespoons olive oil. Clean the tomatoes, cut them into chunks and add them to the onions with a dash of salt and pepper and 1 teaspoon sugar. Cover and cook slowly for 15 minutes. Add the fish and a glass of water. Replace the lid and cook 25 minutes more. Garnish with sprigs of parsley and serve immediately.

800 gr/ 1 3/4 lbs swordfish
  steak, 4 slices
1 onion
4-5 ripe tomatoes
Sugar
Parsley
Olive oil

Servings: 4
Preparation time: 15'
Cooking time: 45'
Difficulty: ●●
Flavor: ●●
Kcal (per serving): 381
Proteins (per serving): 44
Fats (per serving): 16
Nutritional value: ●

Sardine Patties

1 kg/2 lbs fresh sardines
100 gr/4 oz rice for stuffing
4 ripe tomatoes
1 onion
3 cloves garlic
Ground cumin and sweet
  paprika
1 bunch green coriander
Flour
Salt and pepper
Olive oil

Servings: 4
Preparation time: 30'
Cooking time: 35'
Difficulty: ●●
Flavor: ●●●
Kcal (per serving): 439
Proteins (per serving): 35
Fats (per serving): 21
Nutritional value: ●●

Prepare the herbs and vegetables for use; boil the rice for 10 minutes and drain. Open and gut the sardines, eliminate the backbones, heads and tails then put them through the blender with a sprig of coriander and the peeled garlic. Put the mixture into a bowl and blend in the rice, 1 tablespoon paprika, and a pinch each of cumin and salt. Put some flour on your hands, and shape the mixture into little balls, to keep them firm you can add 1 egg white to the mixture.

Gently wilt the chopped onion in a skillet with 2 tablespoons olive oil, add the tomatoes, cut into pieces, salt to taste and reduce the sauce over a low flame for 20 minutes; add the fish balls and cook 15 minutes more. Serve hot with the sauce.

FRIED SARDINES

Squeeze the half lemon. Clean the sardines, eliminating the heads and backbones, open them flat without separating the halves and leave them to dry, open side up. Crush the garlic to a paste. In a bowl combine the finely chopped coriander and parsley, the garlic paste, 1 tablespoon paprika, a pinch of cumin, the lemon juice and a pinch of salt. Beat in the egg and mix to blend well.

Spread the mixture over half the sardines, use the others to cover them. Dredge both sides of each "package" in flour. Fry a few at a time in lots of hot oil, drain on paper towels and season with a light sprinkling of salt. Serve with lettuce, tomato and lemon slices.

1.5 kg/ 3 lbs fresh, medium
  size sardines
1 egg
3 cloves garlic
1 bunch green coriander
  and parsley
Ground cumin and sweet
  paprika
1 and 1/2 lemons (also for
  garnish)
80 gr/3 oz flour
Lettuce and tomatoes
  (for garnish)
Salt
Oil for frying

Servings: 6	
Preparation time: 30'	
Cooking time: 30'	
Difficulty: ●●●	
Flavor: ●●●	
Kcal (per serving): 477	
Proteins (per serving): 33	
Fats (per serving): 31	
Nutritional value: ●●●	

MACKEREL WITH DATES

1 mackerel, about 2 kg/ 2 lbs
100 gr/4 oz farina
150 gr/6 oz shelled almonds
2 dozen dates (use half for
  garnish)
1 egg yolk
Sugar
1 piece ginger root
1 ripe tomato (for garnish)
30 gr/1 oz butter
Olive oil

Servings: 4	
Preparation time: 40'	
Cooking time: 1h	
Difficulty: ●●●	
Flavor: ●●	
Kcal (per serving): 987	
Proteins (per serving): 49	
Fats (per serving): 63	
Nutritional value: ●●●	

1 Cook the farina in a little salted water for 20 minutes, stirring constantly. Remove it from the stove and blend in 1 tablespoon each of butter and sugar, salt and pepper and half the grated ginger root. Let the mixture cool to lukewarm and then blend in the egg yolk.

2 While the mixture is cooling, put the almonds on a baking sheet and toast them at 160°C/325°F, remove the skins, chop them and blend them into the farina mixture.

3 Pit the dates and fill them with the farina mixture.

4 Gut, scale and rinse the fish. Fill the cavity wit the stuffed dates and the rest of the farina mixture. Close with toothpicks and place the mackerel in an oven dish. Season with 3 tablespoons olive oil, salt and pepper and the rest of the grated ginger. Pour 1 glass of water over the mackerel and bake in a preheated oven at 180°C/350°F for 40 minutes. Serve the fish garnished with the rest of the pitted dates and sliced tomato.

FISH KEBABS

1.2 kg/ 2 1/2 lbs bass (or other white Mediterranean fish)
4 ripe tomatoes
2 onions
2 lemons (plus 1 for garnish)
Ground cumin
Bay leaves
Parsley
Olive oil

Servings: 4	
Preparation time: 35'+ 30'	
Cooking time: 20'	
Difficulty: ●●	
Flavor: ●●	
Kcal (per serving): 326	
Proteins (per serving): 37	
Fats (per serving): 13	
Nutritional value: ●	

Combine 12 tablespoons olive oil and the juice of 1 lemon in a bowl, add a pinch each of salt and pepper and 1 tablespoon cumin. Gut, wash, skin and filet the fish; cut it into bite-size pieces and marinate in the oil and lemon juice emulsion for 30 minutes.

Prepare the skewers alternating a piece of fish, tomato wedge, bay leaf, lemon slice and onion. Cook over a charcoal grill or under the broiler for abut 20 minutes, basting often with the marinade. Serve hot, garnished with parsley, bay leaves and lemon slices.

MEATS

Grazing livestock is a vitally important part of Moroccan life, so obviously lamb and mutton have equally important roles as foods. These meats are honored during the feast of Aïd el Kebir . or Aïd el Adha – commemorating the sacrifice of Abraham. It falls on the first day of the month of Muharrem, which is the first day of the Hijrah on the Muslim calendar. Along with ovine meats, there is wide selection of dishes prepared with rabbit, chicken, beef and veal (pork is forbidden by Islamic dietary laws) as you will see in the recipes that follow and complement those Mohammed El Gara has given us in the sections devoted to couscous and tajine.

LAMB WITH PRUNES

1 kg/2 lbs leg of lamb,
  or shoulder
300 gr/12 oz prunes
100 gr/4 oz shelled almonds
1 onion
Cinnamon sticks
Sesame seeds
Honey
80 gr/3 oz butter
Salt and pepper
Olive oil

Servings: 4	
Preparation time: 15' + 30'	
Cooking time: 2h	
Difficulty: ●●	
Flavor: ●●	
Kcal (per serving): 857	
Proteins (per serving): 49	
Fats (per serving): 45	
Nutritional value: ●●●	

1 Soak the prunes in water for 30 minutes. Cut the lamb in to 5 or 6 pieces. Put the meat in a saucepan with 2-3 sticks of cinnamon, the sliced onion, butter, a pinch of salt and 2 glasses of water. Cover and cook slowly for 1 1/2 hours. Remove the lamb, set it aside and keep it warm.

2 Squeeze out the prunes and put them into a pan along with 5 tablespoons honey, 1 teaspoon ground cinnamon and caramelize over a moderate flame.

3 Toast the almonds in a skillet with 3 tablespoons olive oil and toast the sesame seeds in the oven. Serve the meat with the prune sauce and garnished with the almonds and sesame seeds.

RABBIT WITH BEET GREEN STEMS

1 The beet greens should have long, white, tender stems with as little green as possible. Clean the onion and chop it together with the coriander and parsley. Rinse and dry the rabbit, and cut it into 12-14 pieces. Brown the rabbit in a saucepan with 4 tablespoons olive oil and a pinch each of saffron, ginger, salt and pepper; turn the pieces so they cook evenly.

2 When the meat is browned, add the chopped onion, coriander and parsley, cook for 10 minutes to combine the flavors and add about 1 cup hot water. Cover and bring to the boil, then cook slowly for 30 minutes (you can also use a *tajine* to prepare this dish).

3 In the meantime, squeeze the lemon; wash the beet green stems, dry them and remove the leaves (you can boil the leaves separately for a side dish seasoned with olive oil and lemon juice); scrape the stems to remove the "threads" and cut them into 7-8 cm (3 inch) long pieces Put the pieces into a bowl of water and lemon juice. Clean the turnips and cube them.

4 Add the drained stems and turnips to the rabbit, put the lid back on and cook 15 minutes longer – uncover the pan during the last 5 minutes. In the meantime, sauté the almonds in a skillet with a little olive oil. Arrange the rabbit on a serving platter along with the turnips and stems, garnish with the almonds and chopped parsley before serving.

---

1 rabbit, about 1.5 kg/3 lbs, ready to cook
800 gr/ 1 3/4 lbs beet green stems
200 gr/8 oz turnips (see page 45)
50 gr/2 oz shelled, blanched almonds (for garnish)
1 big onion
1 bunch each of green coriander (also for garnish) and parsley
1 lemon
Ground ginger
Powdered saffron
Salt and pepper
Olive oil

Servings: 6	
Preparation time: 30'	
Cooking time: 1h	
Difficulty: ●●	
Flavor: ●●	
Kcal (per serving): 474	
Proteins (per serving): 50	
Fats (per serving): 22	
Nutritional value: ●●	

CHICKEN WITH OLIVES

1 chicken, 1.5 kg/3 lbs, ready
  to cook
250 gr/8 oz green and black
  olives (pitted)
2-3 eggs
1 onion
2 cloves garlic
1 bunch each green coriander
  (also for garnish) and parsley
Ground turmeric and sweet
  paprika
Saffron stems
1 wedge of salted lemon (plus
  a strip of rind for garnish)
1 teaspoon flour
Salt and pepper
Olive oil

Servings: 4-6	
Preparation time: 30'	
Cooking time: 50'	
Difficulty: ●●	
Flavor: ●●	
Kcal (per serving): 733	
Proteins (per serving): 44	
Fats (per serving): 58	
Nutritional value: ●●●	

1 Cook the eggs for 7 minutes, until hardboiled. Shell them when they have cooled. Cut the chicken into about a dozen pieces and rub with 1 clove garlic and a little paprika. Brown the chicken pieces in a saucepan (or *tajine*) with 3 tablespoons olive oil, when they are evenly cooked add the onion chopped together with the other garlic clove, a pinch of turmeric and saffron stems, a level tablespoon paprika and salt and pepper.

2 Cook and stir to combine the flavors, add the chopped coriander and parsley and 1 glass boiling water. Cover and gently bring to the boil and continue cooking for 30 minutes.

3 Add the whole olives, the thinly sliced salted lemon, 1 teaspoon flour, to thicken the sauce and stir, cook uncovered for 10 minutes (add salt and pepper to taste). Serve the chicken hot with the olives and lemon, garnished with sprigs of coriander and strips of lemon rind and the hardboiled eggs cut in half.

STUFFED CHICKEN

1 boned chicken, about 1.2 kg/
  2 1/2 lbs
2 ripe tomatoes
2 stalks celery
1 small zucchini
1 wedge salted lemon
1 clove garlic
1 bunch each green coriander
  and parsley
1 bay leaf
Ground cumin and sweet
  paprika
Mixed steamed vegetables
  (as the side dish)
Salt and pepper
60 gr/2 oz salted butter
  (or *smen*, see page 47)
Olive oil

Servings: 4	
Preparation time: 30'	
Cooking time: 1h 30'	
Difficulty:	●●
Flavor:	●●
Kcal (per serving):	805
Proteins (per serving):	44
Fats (per serving):	65
Nutritional value:	●●●

1 The chicken you order should weigh 1.2 kg/2 1/2 lbs *before* it is boned. Rub it with garlic inside and out and season with salt and pepper. Squeeze the lemon, wash the tomatoes, remove the seeds and dice them.

2 Clean the celery and chop it together with the coriander, parsley and salted lemon. Put the chopped mixture into a bowl, add the tomatoes, the sliced zucchini, 2 tablespoons olive oil, 1/2 tablespoon paprika, a pinch of cumin, the lemon juice and salt and pepper.

3 Mix the vegetables well to combine the ingredients and then stuff the chicken and add 30 gr/1 oz butter. Close with toothpicks, or lace with skewers and kitchen twine.

4 In the bottom portion of the couscous pot, bring about 4 liters/4 quarts of water with the bay leaf and lemon wedge to the boil. Put the chicken in the top portion of the couscous pot and put on the lid. Steam the chicken for 1 hour 20 minutes. Preheat the oven to 200°C/400°F. Melt the rest of the butter and use it to brush the chicken. Place the chicken in an oven dish and put it under the grill for 10 minutes. Serve the crispy chicken with steamed mixed vegetables and little bowls of ground cumin and salt on the side.

Chicken and Olive Patties

500 gr/1 lb chicken or turkey
  breast
200 gr/8 oz green olives (pitted)
1 onion
1 clove garlic
1 lemon
1 egg white
1 bunch each green coriander
  and parsley
Ground cumin, ginger and
  sweet paprika
Saffron stems
30 gr/1 oz flour
Lettuce
Salt and pepper
40 g/1 1/2 oz butter

Servings:	4
Preparation time:	30'
Cooking time:	40'
Difficulty:	●●
Flavor:	●●
Kcal (per serving):	489
Proteins (per serving):	25
Fats (per serving):	37
Nutritional value:	●●

1 Squeeze the lemon. Clean the chicken breast and chop it finely together with the olives, garlic and coriander. Put the mixture into a bowl and combine with the egg white a pinch each of cumin, ginger, salt and pepper.

2 Make about twenty patties and dredge lightly in the flour. Melt the butter in a large skillet and cook the patties until golden (you can also use the *tajine*).

3 In the meantime, clean and chop the onion, add it to the pan with the chicken along with a pinch of saffron stems, 1 tablespoon paprika, a ladle of hot water. Salt to taste.

4 Cover and cook slowly for 30 minutes, then add the chopped parsley and lemon juice, let the sauce reduce over a moderate flame and serve with green salad.

LIVER IN SAVORY SAUCE

600 gr/1 1/2 lb calf liver
12 black olives (pitted, plus
  extra for garnish)
1 big lemon
1 wedge salted lemon
30 gr/1 oz flour
Oil for frying
Olive oil

For the chermoula:
1 bunch each green coriander
  and parsley
Ground cumin and sweet
  paprika
Salt

Servings: 4	
Preparation time: 20'+1h	
Cooking time: 30'	
Difficulty:	●●
Flavor:	●●●
Kcal (per serving): 460	
Proteins (per serving): 31	
Fats (per serving): 33	
Nutritional value:	●●●

1 Prepare the ingredients and squeeze the lemon. To make the *chermoula*: crush the coriander and parsley in a mortar with a pinch of salt. Then, put the paste into a bowl, and blend in a pinch of cumin, 1 tablespoon paprika, half the lemon juice and 1/2 glass of water, pour the *chermoula* into a deep platter.

2 Cut the liver into strips, and put it on top of the *chermoula,* cover and refrigerate for 1 hour.
Drain the liver (keep the *chermoula*), dredge it lightly in flour and fry in a skillet in lots of hot oil. Remove with a slotted spoon when golden, drain on paper towels and cut into little cubes.

3 Pour the marinade into a saucepan, add 3 tablespoons olive oil, 1 glass of hot water and the rest of the lemon juice; boil for 10 minutes.

4 Put the liver pieces into the saucepan, add the olives and the thinly sliced salted lemon, stir and cook briefly and salt to taste. Remove from the stove and serve with the rest of the olives.

MEATBALL KEBABS

900 gr /1 lbs lean chopped
  beef
2 onions
2 cloves garlic
1 bunch each green coriander
  and mint (also for garnish)
Ground cinnamon, cumin and
  sweet paprika
Coriander seeds
Green salad
Salt and pepper

Servings: 6	
Preparation time: 30'	
Cooking time: 15'	
Difficulty: ●	
Flavor: ●●	
Kcal (per serving): 151	
Proteins (per serving): 31	
Fats (per serving): 1	
Nutritional value: ●	

1 Prepare the ingredients: chop the onions together with the garlic, coriander and mint. Mix in a pinch each of cinnamon, cumin and crushed coriander seeds, plus 1 tablespoon paprika.

2 Now add the meat and mix until completely blended, season with salt and pepper.

3 Moisten your hands, take a little of the meat mixture and make an oblong meatball, and wrap it around a skewer. (Metal skewers are best, but wood is fine if it is thick enough). Continue until you have used up all the mixture. Line up the kebabs on a grill over hot, not burning coals (or use the oven grill). Turn them as the meat starts to the brown so that they cook evenly.
Serve the kabobs hot with green salad and sprigs of mint.

900 gr/2 lbs two complete
  lamb livers and lights (heart,
  liver, lungs)
4-5 ovine omentums
Cumin
Salt and pepper

Servings: 6	
Preparation time: 30'	
Cooking time: 20'	
Difficulty: ●	
Flavor: ●●●	
Kcal (per serving): 315	
Proteins (per serving): 24	
Fats (per serving): 22	
Nutritional value: ●●●	

LIVER AND LIGHTS KEBABS

Clean the livers and lights (the trachea which is usually included, is not suited for this dish) and cut them into even pieces, about 2 cm/ 1 inch on a side. Season with salt, pepper and cumin. Soften the omentum by dipping into hot water, spread it on a cutting board and cut squares big enough to wrap around the meat chunks. Stick the little bundles, alternating heart, liver and lungs onto metal or wood skewers. Line up the kebabs on a grill over hot, not burning coals (or use the oven grill) and turn them as each side gets cooked. Serve hot with green salad and sprigs of mint. In western countries it is easier to find pork omentum so that can be used as a substitute.

DESSERTS

Here we are, at the end of our journey through the food
delights that Morocco has to offer. And what could be
a more fitting conclusion than the realm of sweets.
As opposed to European and Western customs, pastries
and biscuits are not confined to the end of the meal.
They are always available to be nibbled at any time.
Moroccan baking is a compendium of all the knowledge
brought over by the early Arab conquerors, creating
the most elegant compositions using basically humble
ingredients. Mohammed El Gara has chosen the best
and most traditional recipes from the endless list of
Moroccan pastries, and also presents his own personal
formula for making a wonderfully fragrant tea,
just like in Morocco.

7

BAGHIR WITH DATES

1 Prepare the batter: combine the sifted flour and semolinaa in a large bowl. In another bowl, dissolve the yeast with a glass of lukewarm water, add the eggs, and a pinch of salt, beat with a whisk to blend. Gradually add the egg mixture to the flour, beating with the whisk, blend in enough lukewarm water to make a smooth, light batter. Cover and set aside in a dry place for 2 hours.

2 In the meantime prepare the filling, pit and chop the dates. Toast the almonds in a dry non-stick pan over a high flame – shaking the pan so the don't burn. Grind the almonds and put them into a bowl, add the dates, 2 teaspoons each cinnamon and orange flower oil.

3 If you do not have a crepe pan, rub a non-stick pan with oil and heat it. Pour a ladleful of batter onto the hot pan, spread it with the bottom of the ladle to get a 15 cm/6 inch diameter crepe that is not too thin. Cook the crepe for about 1 minute and then slide it onto a platter.

4 Repeat until you have used up all the batter; do not overlap the crepes. Distribute the date and almond filling on the crepes, roll up and cut them in half. Serve with honey on the side, or sprinkled with confectioners' sugar, cinnamon and honey.

For the batter
500 gr/1 lb flour
500 gr/1 lb semolina
2 eggs
50 gr/1 1/2 oz brewer's yeast
Salt

For the filling
500 gr/1 lb dates
200 gr/8 oz shelled, blanched
   almonds
Ground cinnamon
Orange flower oil
4 tablespoons honey

Servings: 8-10
Preparation time: 30'+ 2h
Cooking time: 30'
Difficulty: ●
Kcal (per serving): 655
Proteins (per serving): 19
Fats (per serving): 14
Nutritional value: ●●●

BRIOUATS

450 gr/1 lb pastilla dough
(see page 10)
1 kg/2 lbs shelled, blanched
almonds
200 gr/8 oz sugar
1 kg/2 lbs honey
2 eggs
Orange flower oil
Ground cinnamon
80 gr/3 oz sesame seeds
(for garnish)
Flour (for the worktable)
30 gr/1 oz butter
Oil for frying

Servings: 8-10	
Preparation time: 40'	
Cooking time: 30'	
Difficulty: ●●●	
Kcal (per serving): 1487	
Proteins (per serving): 31	
Fats (per serving): 85	
Nutritional value: ●●●	

1 Toast 250 gr/8 oz almonds in a skillet with a drop of oil until golden, drain and chop finely. Put the rest of the almonds through the blender with the sugar; run the blender at low speed until you get a smooth paste. Put the almond paste into a bowl, add the golden, chopped almonds, the butter, 2 tablespoons orange flower water and 2 teaspoons cinnamon. Work the mixture until it is smoothly blended.

2 Separate the eggs. Cut the sheets of dough into 10 cm/4 inch wide strips; put a little of the almond mixture on the bottom edge of each strip. Fold up the corner and brush with egg white.

3 Continue folding the dough upwards in triangles and brushing with egg white. When the *briouats* are closed, brush with slightly beaten egg yolk and fry a few at a time in lots of hot oil. Remove when golden using a slotted spoon and drain on paper towels.

4 Heat the honey over a low flame, or in a double boiler, until it is fluid. Using tongs dip each *briouat* into the honey, let the excess drip off, arrange them on a platter and sprinkle with sesame seeds. Another delicious filling is rice boiled in milk with almonds.

SWEET COUSCOUS

1 kg/1 lbs fine grain couscous
  (*seffa*, see page 46)
200 gr/8 oz shelled, blanched
  almonds
3 dl/ 2/3 cup milk
  (plus extra to drink)
1 lemon
Confectioners' sugar
Ground cinnamon
Orange flower oil
  (to flavor the milk)
75 gr/3 oz butter
Peanut oil

Servings: 8	
Preparation time: 40'	
Cooking time: 1h 10'	
Difficulty: ●●●	
Kcal (per serving): 814	
Proteins (per serving): 21	
Fats (per serving): 35	
Nutritional value: ●●●	

1 Spread the couscous in a large concave plate, mix and moisten with a little water and 1 tablespoon oil; put it in the top portion of the couscous pot. In the bottom portion bring 4 liters/4 quarts of water with the lemon cut into wedges to the boil.

2 Fit the couscous over boiling water, steam for 20 minutes. Turn it onto the plate and mix, added 1/3 of the milk and butter. Let it rest for 5 minutes, put it back to steam for another 20 minutes. Turn it onto the plate and mix again with 1/3 of the milk and butter; steam for 20 minutes.

3 In the meantime, gently brown the almonds in a pan with a little oil; remove with a slotted spoon and drain on paper towels. Put the couscous on the serving platter, mix in the rest of the milk and butter. Shape it into a dome and decorate it with sprinkled confectioner's sugar and cinnamon – make any pretty pattern you like – and put the chopped almonds in the middle. Serve with cold milk flavored with orange flower oil.

GAZELLE HORNS

250 gr/8 oz flour (plus extra for the worktable and pan)
500 gr/1 lb shelled, blanched almonds
250 gr/8 oz sugar
Ground cinnamon
1 piece of lemon rind
2 dl/ 3/4 cup orange flower oil
Confectioners' sugar (optional)
Salt
50 gr/ 1 1/2 oz butter
Peanut oil

Servings:	4-6
Preparation time:	40'+ 15'
Cooking time:	15'
Difficulty:	●●
Kcal (per serving):	987
Proteins (per serving):	23
Fats (per serving):	63
Nutritional value:	●●●

Combine the flour with half the butter, a pinch of salt, half the orange flower oil and enough lukewarm water to make a dough the consistency of bread dough. Shape it into a ball and set it aside.

Put the almonds, sugar and lemon rind through the blender to make a paste. Put it into a bowl and blend in the rest of the orange flower oil, 1 teaspoon cinnamon and the rest of the butter mixing by hand to get smooth consistency.

Grease a plate with oil; take a small amount of the almond mixture, roll it back and forth on the plate to make a "sausage" 5-6 cm/ 2 inches long and 1.5 cm/ 1/2 inches wide. Continue until you have used up all the mixture and keep the "almond sausages" from overlapping.

Heat the oven to 160°C/320°F. Roll out the dough very thinly on a floured surface. Cut strips 20 cm/8 inches long by 6 cm/2 inches wide. Line up the "almond sausage" on top of each one, roll up the dough and seal the ends by pressing down. Separate and trim with a pastry cutter, use the scraps to make more strips to wrap the "sausages," and continue until you have used up all the ingredients. Bend the rolls slightly, to make curved "gazelle horns," place them on a floured baking sheet and bake for 15 minutes. If you like, you can dust them with confectioners' sugar before serving.

HONEY FRITTERS

250 gr/8 oz flour
1 potato, boiled in the jacket
20 gr/1 oz brewer's yeast
100 gr/4 oz sesame seeds
1 glass milk
150 gr/6 oz honey
Vegetable oil for frying

Servings: 4	
Preparation time: 45' + 2h	
Cooking time: 40'	
Difficulty: ●●	
Kcal (per serving): 692	
Proteins (per serving): 8	
Fats (per serving): 28	
Nutritional value: ●●●	

Peel and mash the potato, combine it with the flour, a pinch of salt and the yeast, diluted in lukewarm water. Gradually add the milk which should be at room temperature.
Cover the bowl and set aside to rise for 1 hour. Knead it again and set it aside to rise for another hour. Make little balls and fry them in hot oil; drain on paper towels. Heat the honey in a sauce pan, use tongs to dip the fritters into the liquefied honey and then roll them in sesame seeds.

FAKKAS

1 Soak the raisins in lukewarm water for 30 minutes before you begin. Toast the sesame seeds and the almonds separately in dry, non-stick pans over a lively flame. Chop 3/4 of the almonds, leave the rest whole.

2 In a large bowl, beat the 8 eggs with the sugar until light and creamy, blend in 100 gr/4 oz softened butter. Then mix in the chopped and whole almonds, the squeezed out raisins and 1 teaspoon orange flower oil.

3 Dissolve the yeast in a little lukewarm water and mix it with the flour, add this to the egg mixture and blend with a wire whisk (or mixer) until you have a smooth, elastic dough. Cover the dough put it in a warm, not hot, place to rise for 2 hours. Heat the oven to 180°C/350°F.

4 Knead the dough to soften it and shape it into orange-size balls. Flatten the balls on a floured surface and roll out little loaves that are 20 cm/8 inches long, 3 cm/ 1 inch thick and 5 cm/2 inches wide.
Brush the loaves with beaten egg yolk diluted with a little water. Place them on a buttered and floured baking sheet and bake for 25 minutes. Remove from the oven and while still warm, cut the loaves into 1 cm (1/2 inch) thick slices; bake these slices for 15 minutes more and enjoy these golden biscuits with tea.

1 kg/2 lbs flour (plus extra for
  worktable and pan)
8 eggs and 1 yolk
250 gr/8 oz sugar
200 gr/8 oz raisins
200 gr/8 oz shelled, blanched
  almonds
80 gr/3 oz sesame seeds
30 gr/1 oz brewer's yeast
Orange flower oil
120 gr/4 1/4 oz butter
Olive oil

Servings: 8-10	
Preparation time: 35'+ 2h	
Cooking time: 40'	
Difficulty: ●●	
Kcal (per serving): 925	
Proteins (per serving): 24	
Fats (per serving): 41	
Nutritional value: ●●●	

Walnut Ghriba

1.2 kg/2 1/2 lbs shelled
  walnuts
250 gr/8 oz sugar
4 eggs
1 strip lemon rind
ground cinnamon
orange flower oil (for your
  hands)
30 gr/1 oz confectioners' sugar
80 gr/3 oz butter

Servings:	8-10
Preparation time:	35'+ 2h
Cooking time:	40'
Difficulty:	●
Kcal (per serving):	806
Proteins (per serving):	24
Fats (per serving):	66
Nutritional value:	●●●

1 Finely chop 1 kg/2 lbs of the walnuts. Beat the eggs and sugar (use a wire whisk or electric mixer) until light and frothy.

2 Add the chopped walnuts, 60 gr/2 oz butter, 1 teaspoon cinnamon, the finely grated lemon peel and the confectioners' sugar, blend until you have a smooth mixture. Heat the oven to 160°C/325°F.

3 Moisten your hands with orange flower oil – this is one of Mohammed El Gara's little secrets. Take a little dough and shape round, slightly flattened biscuits; decorate each one with half a walnut. Put them on a buttered baking sheet and bake for 20 minutes. Cool before serving.

Coffee is usually prepared Turkish style, that is an infusion with no need for a percolator or other coffee maker. The beans are ground very finely, so they dissolve right in the glass. People do not drink coffee in a rush or standing up, it is a beverage to enjoy seated and talking to friends. Often it is flavored with cinnamon, orange flower oil or spices such as anise, cardamom, ginger or nutmeg which is typical of Marrakech and southern Morocco.

TEA AND COFFEE

10 gr/ 1 teaspoon per person,
fine-leaf green tea
1 bunch mint leaves
sugar (optional)

Serving: 6
Preparation time: 10'
Cooking time: 5'

In Morocco people drink tea any time of day, alone or in company, with guests and friends. Any occasion is good for enjoying its aroma and flavor. Preparing tea in Morocco is a little ceremony as Mohammed El Gara explains: first of all you need a metal teapot – or one that can be put on the stove. Put 1 teaspoon of tea-leaves for each person into the pot. Add 1 tablespoon boiling water, shake the teapot vigorously and discard the water – not the tea!. Repeat. Add the mint leaves (the best and most fragrant come from Meknès), fill the teapot with warm water, add sugar to your liking and heat the water until it boils. Pour the tea into glasses from higher than you usually would, creating a "frothy head." This "airs" the tea and removes the acidity. Enjoy the tea hot, with biscuits or cakes, or just plain. Some people like it without mint, or with other flavors such as absinthe, sage, verbena, marjoram, basil or orange flower.

ALMOND SNAKE

Put the almonds through the blender with the sugar. Melt the butter and combine half with the almonds, blend in 1 teaspoon cinnamon and 1 of orange flower oil, and mix until you have a malleable dough. Heat the oven to 160°C/325°F. Line up the sheets of dough on a floured surface so that the edges overlap slightly, brush with egg white. Shape the almond paste into a long sausage and put it in the middle of the dough. Roll up the dough make a tube that you can twist into a spiral. Grease a round oven pan with oil, put the dough in it and brush with the remaining melted butter. Bake for 30 minutes. In the meantime, liquefy the honey over a low flame. When the cake it done spread the liquefied honey over it.

200 gr/8 oz pastilla dough
 (see page 10)
500 gr/1 lb shelled, blanched
 almonds
250 gr/8 oz sugar
150 gr/6 oz honey
Orange flower oil
Ground cinnamon
1 egg white
Flour (for the worktable)
70 gr/ 2 1/2 oz butter
Olive oil

Servings: 6	
Preparation time: 25'	
Cooking time: 25'	
Difficulty: ●●●	
Kcal (per serving): 1072	
Proteins (per serving): 23	
Fats (per serving): 66	
Nutritional value: ●●●	

SFOUF

600 gr/21 oz flour
600 gr/ 21 oz shelled, blanched almonds (plus extra for garnish)
500 gr/1 lb sesame seeds
500 gr/1 lb honey
Ground cinnamon (also for garnish)
Nutmeg
Anise seeds
Orange flower water
Confectioners' sugar (for garnish)
200 gr/8 oz butter
Olive oil

Servings: 6	
Preparation time: 30'	
Cooking time: 10'	
Difficulty: ●●	
Kcal (per serving): 1510	
Proteins (per serving): 34	
Fats (per serving): 94	
Nutritional value: ●●●	

1 Set the oven thermostat to 200°C/400°F. Spread the flour in an oven pan and toast until lightly golden, then sift it. Toast the sesame seeds in a dry pan over a lively flame.

2 Toast the almonds in another pan with a little oil, remove with a slotted spoon and drain on paper towels.

3 Combine 1/3 of the toasted sesame seeds with the almonds and put through the blender. Put the mixture into a bowl and blend in the flour, 2 tablespoons cinnamon, a pinch of ground nutmeg, a pinch of crushed anise seeds, 2 tablespoons orange flower oil and the liquefied honey.

4 Add the melted butter and continue blending until smooth. Shape into a dome or pyramid and cover with the remaining toasted sesame seeds and decorate with almonds, cinnamon and confectioners' sugar and let it harden.